Tons of Scientifically Provocative and Socially Acceptable Things to Do with Balloons under the Guise of Teaching Science

Tons of Scientifically Provocative and Socially Acceptable Things to Do with Balloons under the Guise of Teaching Science

by
Glenn McGlathery
and
Larry Malone

Illustrations by
Sue Ware

1991
TEACHER IDEAS PRESS
A Division of
Libraries Unlimited, Inc.
Englewood, Colorado

TEACHER IDEAS PRESS
A Division of
Libraries Unlimited, Inc.
P.O. Box 6633
Englewood, CO 80155-6633

Library of Congress Cataloging-in-Publication Data

McGlathery, Glenn, 1934-
    Tons of scientifically provocative and socially acceptable things
to do with balloons under the guise of teaching science / by Glenn
McGlathery and Larry Malone ; illustrations by Sue Ware.
    xiv, 141 p. 22x28 cm.
    Includes bibliographical references (p. 139).
    ISBN 0-87287-783-3
    1. Science--Study and teaching (Elementary) 2. Balloons.
3. Creative activities and seat work. I. Malone, Larry, 1943-
II. Title.
LB1585.M37   1991
372.3'5044--dc20   90-20667
                                                              CIP

Table of Contents

Preface

Balloons are a lot of fun in and of themselves, but we had more in mind than introducing a few activities to teachers and others in which the ever-popular balloons are featured. The activities featured in this book illustrate a variety of science concepts, including air pressure, chemical reactions, density, elasticity, gravity, heat, propulsion, and static electricity. One concept is discussed in an expository form at the beginning of each chapter of the book. These mini-essays are "explaining" sections rather than "doing" sections. Some people are anxious to know why certain things happen. Others don't really care and just want to have fun messing around with stuff. We've tried to accommodate both types, those who ponder and those who putter. For those who require greater insight into scientific phenomena exposed by the demonstrations, check the bibliography for more complete sources of information. If you are the hands-on type, the world is your balloon, and we hope this book will provide you with numerous points of departure into fun and discovery.

Acknowledgments

Many people are responsible for this book, and we are indebted to them for their ideas, encouragement, and help. In particular, we thank our friend, Linda De Lucchi of the Lawrence Hall of Science at the University of California at Berkeley, whose friendship, patience, and insight are much appreciated. Bobby Jones of the University of Houston at Clear Lake City, Texas gave us many ideas and practical help. Teachers and students in many of our classes and in other settings were valuable in their willingness to try many of the activities in their classrooms and to provide useful feedback.

Introduction: A Short History and Other Miscellany Concerning Toy Balloons

ABOUT BALLOONS ...

Balloons are a common sight in our world. We see children and adults carrying balloons at the zoo, in the park, in malls, at fairs and store openings, at birthday parties, at school dances, at carnivals, and just about everywhere you look. Balloons symbolize happiness and are a hallmark of a celebration. "Bouquets" of balloons are often sent as gifts. I'm almost always on the lookout for balloons and seldom a day goes by without my seeing at least one.

Balloons have been around to fascinate people for a long time. The first balloons were found over 2,000 years ago in China. These balloons were made of paper and often highly decorated. The art in which we see these Chinese balloons shows them to be used by acrobats, so we don't know if they were widely used by children. Japanese origami, the art of folding paper to make various forms, can produce a paper globe that can be filled with air. Some people have used organs of animals to make "balloons." For example, Eskimos have used the inflated bladders of seals as floats in their activities on the water.

Indians of Central and South America made balloons by dipping gourds into raw latex from the rubber tree. The thin layer of latex that stuck to the gourd was "cured" over a fire, then the "balloon" was peeled off.

An important discovery by Charles Goodyear in 1839 made the toy balloon a common product. Goodyear discovered a process called vulcanization in which latex and sulfur are mixed, then cured, in a hot oven. Vulcanization makes it possible to have very thin yet strong and elastic balloons. Children were able to buy vulcanized balloons at circuses and fairs for a penny each in the 1800s.

Now balloons are made by dipping aluminum forms into latex that has been colored. The forms are "cured" in an oven, stripped from the mold, and washed. If the balloons are to be printed, they are reinflated. Today, over a billion balloons are sold each year.

BUYING BALLOONS

Balloons come in all qualities. Generally, you get what you pay for. Balloons bought in discount department stores are pretty inexpensive but not always of the best quality. There are stores that specialize in balloons. That's where you will probably get the best balloons. Usually, balloons sold in a balloon specialty store are of good quality to start with and are fresh and well kept. The turnover and resupply in such a store usually ensures the quality. Balloons that are carefully stored can have a shelf life of up to a year, but balloons that are carelessly stocked can deteriorate in as little as two months.

Of course balloons come in different colors and sizes, but they also come in different strengths. The two main types of toy balloons are spherical and cylindrical. Spherical balloons can be ordered by their inflated diameter sizes (7-inch, 8-inch, 12-inch, etc.). Cylindrical balloons are coded with three-digit numbers. The first digit indicates how large in diameter the inflated balloon will be. The next two digits indicate how long the inflated balloon will be. For example, a balloon with the number 312 will inflate into a cylinder 3 inches in diameter and 12 inches long. The balloons that are used to make toy animals are often #260. This balloon will inflate to only a 2-inch diameter but will be about 60 inches or five feet long. Additionally, a letter *A* or *E* can be included after the numbers. *A* means that the balloon is thin enough to be fairly easily inflated. *E* is a designation for entertainer grade, a much tougher balloon to inflate. People who use balloons frequently have developed techniques for inflating *E*-grade balloons. This technique is discussed at the end of this introduction under "Inflating Balloons."

This information on numbering may be too technical for most people, who just see a balloon they want and buy it. But some people will want to shop for just the right balloon and enjoy going to a specialty store and asking for exactly what they want.

STORING BALLOONS

Balloons are sensitive to heat and light. Either of these can dramatically shorten the life of balloons. Ozone is as large enemy of balloons. This gas in our atmosphere causes very small holes in the walls of balloons, a real problem in most of the applications for balloons. Heat is a larger problem. Heat causes aging, weakening the wall. This results often in the balloon bursting when you try to inflate it.

The best way to store balloons is in a closed container away from heat and sunlight. They don't have to be in a refrigerator or freezer but they will last longer in a cool place. If the balloons are going to be stored for a long time it's a good idea to sprinkle a little cornstarch in with them. This prevents the balloons from sticking together. If you neglect your balloons for a long period of time, you will sometimes open a package and find that they are all stuck together. After balloons have fused this way, they are of no use whatsoever.

INFLATING BALLOONS

Inflating balloons can be very difficult for some people. It's always a good idea to stretch the balloon several times before you try to inflate it. This makes the rubber a little more pliable. People who work with balloons a lot develop little tricks for inflating. A common trick is to use the cheek muscles to get the balloons started, then take a breath and use the chest and diaphragm muscles to complete the job. Some people use an air pump to inflate balloons. These pumps can be bought at most balloon stores or you can use a hand pump for your balloons by devising some kind of adaptor. For example, the metal fitting on the hose of a bicycle tire pump could be cut off and the hose pushed through a one-hole rubber stopper that tapered to a ½-inch (12- to 13-mm) diameter, over which the mouth of the balloon to be inflated could be stretched.

Air Pressure

CONCEPT OF AIR PRESSURE

The activities in the chapter "Air Pressure" illustrate some facets of the concept of air pressure. We are probably most familiar with the term *air pressure* from radio and television weather broadcasts. The announcer may state that the air pressure is 29.75 inches. What does that mean?

First of all, it is important to remember that air has mass (weight). Air occupies space from the ground to the upper reaches of our atmosphere, about 80 miles. Imagine that you are playing a game of "pile on." If you are on the bottom of the pile, the pressure on you is the sum of the weight of the players above you. Air can be thought of as billions and billions of air molecules in blocks playing pile on. It should be noted that there is less air in each subsequent piled-up block, and the blocks at the top are practically empty and weightless.

Visualize cubic-foot blocks of air stacked on top of each other. Each cubic foot of air weighs just about .08 pounds at sea level. That doesn't seem like too much; it would take more than 12 cubic feet of air to weigh a pound. But if you consider that there are lots of cubic feet stacked on top of each other to reach the limits of our atmosphere (almost a half million), and the pressure at the bottom (surface of the earth) is due to the weight of all these blocks, we are, all of a sudden, talking about some real pressure.

Air pressure is affected by a number of factors. For example, warm air is less dense than cold air. As heat is added to the air, the molecules become more active, pushing each other further apart. Warmed air expands (if not confined) and cooled air contracts. Warm air has fewer molecules per unit volume, so it exerts less pressure on the earth than cool air. If, however, warm air is trapped in a closed container, such as a balloon or a can, the increased activity of the molecules will increase the pressure on the inside of the container. The balloon inflates because the rubber can be stretched. The can can't stretch very much so pressure inside it builds up.

So back to the weather announcer.... Air pressure is measured with an instrument called a barometer. Torricelli, an assistant of Galileo, discovered the principle of the barometer in the seventeenth century. How does it work? Imagine a bowl of liquid and a tube sealed at one end inverted in it so that the open end is below the surface of the liquid. Imagine that the tube has no air or any other gas in it. Air pressure will push liquid up into the tube until the weight of the liquid in the tube is equivalent to the weight of a column of air of the same cross section from that point to the limits of our atmosphere. The weight of such a column of air with a cross-sectional area of 1 square inch is about 14.7 pounds. If water is used as the liquid, the height of a column of water supported by air pressure is about 34 feet. A denser liquid will require a shorter tube. Mercury, a metal over 13 times more dense than water, will be pushed up about 30 inches. So, if the meteorologist reports barometric pressure of 29.75 inches, she means that the air pressure at that time is supporting a column of mercury 29.75 inches high.

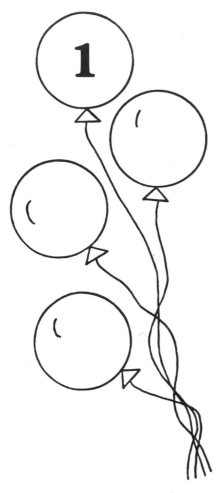

Shhhh!!!
The Balloons Have Ears

Materials

Balloon, 7-inch to 9-inch, round

Plastic tumblers (2)

Hot and cold running water

Preparation

This activity requires hot and cold running water. Normal tap water should suffice. It's a good idea to try this by yourself before you show it to someone else so you get a feel for how long to "heat" the tumblers and how long to "cool" them.

Activity

Inflate and tie off the balloon. Heat the tumblers by running hot water over them. Press the rims of the tumblers tightly onto opposite sides of the balloon. While holding them tightly against the balloon, cool the tumblers by running cold water over them. "Ears" form as the tumblers stick to the balloon. A seal is formed that will hold the tumblers to the balloon so tightly that the balloon will wear the tumblers like ear muffs. A silly face drawn on the balloon enhances this activity immensely.

Science Concepts and Principles

Heating the tumblers with the warm, running water causes the air molecules in the tumblers to become more active. When cold water is run on the tumblers they cool and so does the air trapped inside them. The cooled air contracts, resulting in a partial vacuum. The greater air pressure outside the tumblers holds them tightly against the balloon, resulting in the unlikely "eared" balloon. If you use just one tumbler (for a nose), you can make quite a satisfactory pig face with your felt tip pen. And with three tumblers....

The Stubborn Balloon

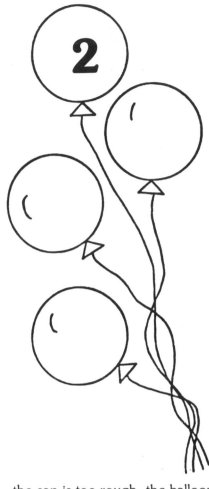

Materials

Small balloon

Soup-size tin can, open at one end, with small hole punched on the side near the bottom

Soapy water

Tools

Hammer

Sixteen-penny nail

Sandpaper

Preparation

Punch a hole in the side of the can near the bottom, using the nail and hammer. Check the rim of the open end of the can. Use sandpaper to smooth off rough edges if necessary. If the rim of the can is too rough, the balloon will burst as you try this activity. This is certainly not desirable if you are trying to impress someone.

Prepare soapy water by putting a little dishwashing detergent in a glass of water. Apply a little soapy water to the mouth of the can. Inflate the balloon until it is just slightly larger than the diameter of the can and tie it off.

Activity

Ask a friend to try to stuff the balloon inside a can. As he or she tries to do it, secretly hold your finger over the hole in the can. Your friend can't do it, even using soapy water as a lubricant. State that it's really easy to do, then secretly remove your finger from the hole. You will easily push the balloon inside the can.

Science Concepts and Principles

The balloon will not go into the can when the hole is covered, because the balloon seals the can opening and traps a volume of air inside. The trapped air has no place to go. The harder your friend pushes, the greater the pressure exerted by the air in the can to keep the balloon out. The balloon goes into the can when the hole is open because the trapped air escapes through the hole, allowing space for the balloon to enter.

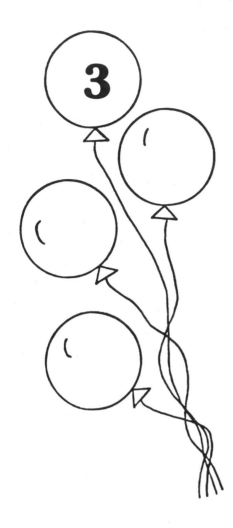

The Inside-Out Balloon

Materials

Balloon, 7-inch

Plastic funnel, 3-inch

Tools

Scissors

Preparation

You may want to cut off the neck of the balloon before you demonstrate this activity, although the cutting is so easily accomplished you can do it as part of the demonstration. Just remember to do it with a little flourish.

Activity

Cut the neck off the balloon. Fit the neckless balloon over the mouth (wide end) of a small funnel. Suck air out of the funnel. As air is sucked out, the balloon turns inside out and goes into the funnel.

Science Concepts and Principles

Air exerts pressure on both sides of the balloon membrane stretched across the funnel, both inside and out. This is because air is free to flow through the funnel stem. As you suck on the stem of the funnel, you remove some of the air that was inside of the balloon. A partial vacuum results. Now there is more pressure outside the funnel than inside. The balloon collapses into the funnel. Some students might think you are sucking the balloon into the funnel, but in reality air pressure is **pushing** the balloon down into the funnel.

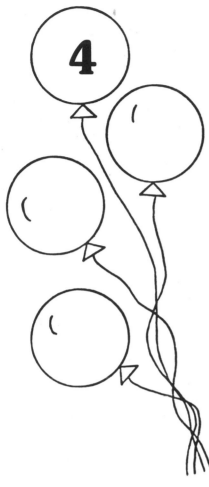

A Balloon Trick

Materials

Balloon, 7-inch

Plastic tumbler, 12-ounce to 16-ounce

Water

Preparation

Try this activity ahead of time. It takes a little practice to blow up a balloon inside a tumbler, and it also takes a little practice to know when the balloon has expanded enough to form a seal tight enough to allow the tumbler to be lifted.

Activity

Fill the tumbler about one-third full of water. Hold the balloon in the tumbler as you inflate it. The balloon expands against the tumbler and holds so tightly that the tumbler of water can be raised when you lift the balloon by its stem.

Science Concepts and Principles

The balloon forms a seal against the inside wall of the tumbler as it expands. Eventually, the force of the seal is sufficient to allow the tumbler to be lifted.

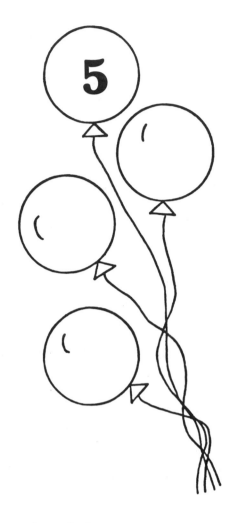

Balloon in a Bottle

Materials

Balloon, 7-inch

Bottle with a 1½-inch opening

Matches

Newspaper squares about 4 inches by 4 inches

Preparation

Try this activity by yourself before you attempt to demonstrate it for someone else. It takes a little practice to know how long to let the paper burn before placing the balloon over the bottle. It also takes a little practice to stretch quickly a small-necked balloon over a large-necked bottle when there is a fire burning close at hand.

Activity

Tear a strip of newspaper about 4 inches by 4 inches. Accordion pleat the paper so it will pass easily into the bottle. Light the paper with a match and drop the burning paper inside the bottle. Immediately stretch the neck of the balloon over the bottle. The balloon will be sucked into the bottle.

Science Concepts and Principles

The fire in the bottle heats the air. Heated air expands. When you place the balloon on the bottle the heated air inside the bottle is trapped. As this volume of air cools it contracts creating a partial vacuum. The outside air pressure pushes the balloon into the region of lower pressure.

Betcha Can't!

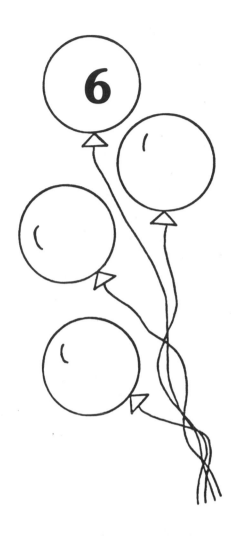

Materials

Balloon, 7-inch

Glass pop bottle, 6-ounce to 10-ounce size

Soda straw

Rubber band

Modeling clay, a walnut-sized ball

Masking tape

Tools

Scissors

Preparation

Cut the lip off the balloon with a pair of scissors. Put the soda straw about ½ inch inside the balloon. Tightly wrap the tip of the balloon around the straw and tape with a piece of masking tape.

Activity

Wrap the clay around the middle of the straw and insert the straw into the bottle with the balloon **inside**. Use clay to make an airtight seal between the straw and the bottle. Try to inflate the balloon by blowing into the straw. You can inflate the balloon only a small amount, regardless of how hard you blow.

Science Concepts and Principles

The bottle is filled with air when the balloon is inserted. In order to inflate the balloon you would need to move aside the air inside the bottle. Because the trapped air has no place to go the only way you could possible inflate the balloon would be to blow hard enough so that the air in the bottle would compress. You're not able to compress this air very much at all, so you simply cannot inflate the balloon.

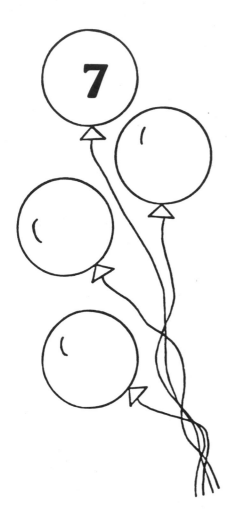

Warming Up

Materials

Balloon, 7-inch to 9-inch

Tape measure

Candle

Matches

Preparation

No advanced preparation is required, although it is wise to try the activity yourself before demonstrating it to others. We've found that some people are quite put off by the smell of burning rubber.

Activity

Inflate the balloon and tie it off. Carefully measure the circumference with a tape measure. Bring a lighted candle close (careful!) to the balloon for a minute or so. Remeasure the circumference of the balloon. You will find the balloon has enlarged.

Science Concepts and Principles

Heating the air in the balloon increases the speed of the molecules. This results in greater pressure exerted on the balloon and it will expand and allow the air to expand.

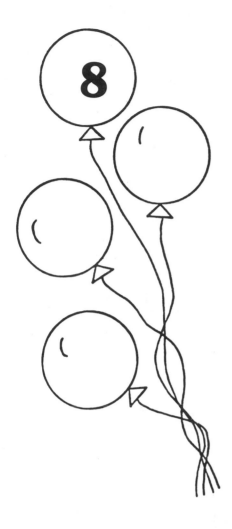

The Incredible Nonshrinking Balloon

Materials

Balloon, 7-inch to 9-inch

Glass pop bottle, 1 quart size, if possible

Saucepan, deep, if possible

Hot water

Preparation

No advanced preparation is necessary other than finding the materials needed to do this activity. It's always a good idea, however, to try an activity like this one by yourself before demonstrating it to others. You may envision a tremendous expansion as you read about this activity. Don't be disappointed. The concept will be demonstrated but not in an **exaggerated** fashion.

Activity

Stretch the neck of a balloon over the neck of a glass pop bottle. Stand the bottle in very hot water. Observe what happens to the balloon.

Science Concepts and Principles

The air inside the pop bottle is at or near room temperature when the activity begins. Heating the air in the bottle increases the speed of the molecules. This results in greater pressure exerted on the balloon and it will expand to allow the air to expand.

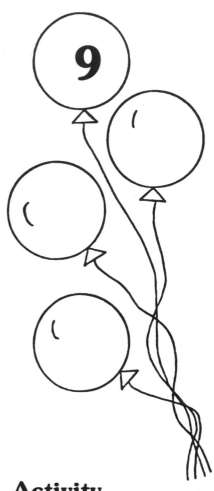

The Incredible Shrinking Balloon

Materials

Long balloon

Tape measure

Refrigerator with freezer compartment (Don't buy one just for this activity; you can probably find one that you can use.)

Preparation

Results are not always "dramatic." Practice measuring the circumference with the tape measure, as this is not an easy task.

Activity

Inflate the balloon and tie it off. Measure the circumference of the balloon. Put the balloon in the freezer compartment of the refrigerator for 30 minutes. Remove the balloon from the refrigerator and remeasure its circumference. The circumference will be smaller.

Science Concepts and Principles

The air in the balloon is at or close to room temperature when it is first inflated, perhaps slightly warmer depending on how much hot air you use to inflate the balloon. Cooling the air in the balloon decreases the speed of the molecules. This results in less pressure exerted on the inside of the balloon and it contracts as the air contracts.

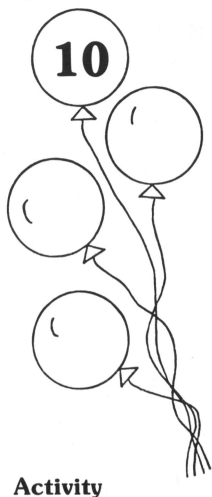

The Credible Shrinking Balloons

Materials

Balloons, 7-inch

Cloth tape measure

Felt tip marker (black is best)

Pencil

Piece of paper

Refrigerator/freezer needs to be available

Preparation

No advanced preparation is necessary. This activity takes a little time, at least 30 minutes for the inflated balloons to be placed in their new environments.

Activity

Use the felt tip marker to number the balloons 1, 2, and 3. Inflate the balloons to the same size and tie off the ends. Measure the circumference of each balloon and record it. Put balloon 1 on a shelf at room temperature. Put balloon 2 in the refrigerator, and balloon 3 in the freezer. After 30 minutes, measure the circumference of each balloon and record the data in a table like the one following.

	Circumference at room temp.	Circumference later
Balloon #1		
Balloon #2		
Balloon #3		

Science Concepts and Principles

Air expands when heated and contracts when cooled if the container it is in allows it. The rubber container (balloon) responds to the pressure changes and will contract when the air inside it contracts.

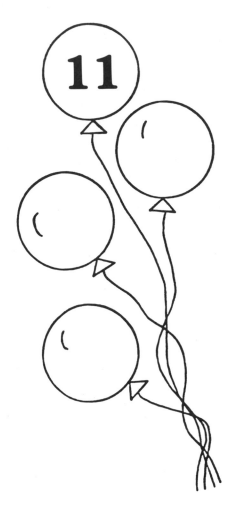

The Old Balloon-in-the-Bottle Trick

Materials

Balloon, 7-inch
Bottle with 1½-inch opening
Matches
Newspaper squares about 4 inches by 4 inches
Cooking oil or petroleum jelly

Preparation

Fill the balloon with water until it is slightly larger than the mouth of the bottle. Tie it off. It's easier to get the balloon to go into the bottle if the balloon is smaller, but that's no big deal for the onlookers. You may recognize this activity as a thinly disguised "egg-in-a-bottle trick" in which a peeled, hard-boiled egg is used instead of the balloon. But, hey, this book is about balloons. When we do the book on eggs watch for the old egg-in-the-bottle trick.

You need to practice this trick a couple of times before you do it in front of an audience. You may find that it helps to put a little cooking oil or petroleum jelly around the mouth of the bottle.

Activity

Accordion pleat a small square of newspaper. Light the paper with a match and drop it into the bottle. Immediately place the water balloon over the mouth of the bottle and watch as it is pushed into the bottle.

Science Concepts and Principles

The fire in the bottle heats the air. Heated air expands. When you place the water balloon on top of the bottle the heated air is trapped. As this volume of air cools, the speed of the molecules is reduced, resulting in reduced pressure. The air pressure outside the bottle pushes the balloon into the region of lower pressure. Would the trick work if we waited several minutes after the paper was lighted before we put the balloon on top of the bottle? No, it wouldn't, because the heated air in the bottle would have time to cool so that when you put the balloon on the bottle the air pressure outside and inside the balloon would be so nearly the same that the water balloon would not be pushed in.

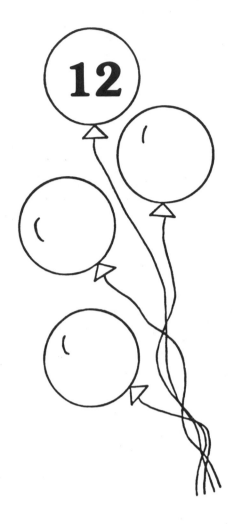

The Old Balloon-out-of-the-Bottle Trick

Materials

Same as those needed for the old balloon-in-the-bottle trick described previously.

Preparation

Do the old balloon-in-the-bottle trick (page 12).

Activity

Now that the balloon is in the bottle, challenge an innocent observer to get the balloon out of the bottle, keeping both the balloon and the bottle intact. When the best have given up, simply tip the bottle up so that the balloon slides down the neck. Keep the neck tilted upward as you put the bottle to your lips and blow as hard as you can into the bottle. Stop blowing and watch the balloon slide out into your hand as slick as you please.

Science Concepts and Principles

Again, it's air pressure that does the work for you. By blowing hard into the bottle, air is forced past the balloon into the bottle, and pressure greater than ambient air pressure results. The balloon acts like a valve, sealing the bottle so that no air can get past. The pressure inside pushes on the balloon until the pressure is the same inside and out. Usually the balloon is pushed out of the bottle before this happens.

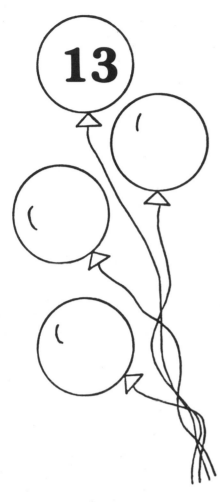

Hot and Cold

Materials

Balloon, 7-inch

Pop bottle

Pan filled with ice water

Preparation

Try this activity by yourself before you try it with someone else so you can see how long changes take. Depending on a number of factors, this demonstration can be really **slow**. In cases like this, have a clever repartee ready to go. For example, "Did you hear about the balloon that was so liberated that she wanted to be filled with **her**lium rather than **he**lium?" Maybe you can do better. Sure, you can do better.

Activity

Inflate the balloon to about 1½ inches in diameter. Stretch the neck of the balloon over the mouth of the pop bottle. Next, put the bottle in a pan filled with ice water. Observe what happens. The balloon will contract, sometimes ending up inside the bottle.

Science Concepts and Principles

Air expands when heated and contracts when cooled, if the container allows it. The cooling of the air in the system decreases the speed of the molecules. This results in reduced pressure exerted on the inside of the balloon and it will contract as the air inside contracts. If there is enough difference between air at room temperature and the air cooled inside the balloon, the change can be dramatic. Sometimes the balloon will end up inside the bottle.

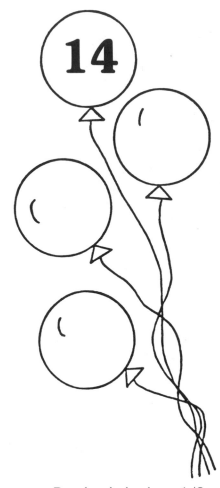

Soup Can Trick

Materials

Soup can
Balloon, 7-inch to 9-inch
Rubber band

Tools

Sixteen-penny nail
Hammer
Scissors

Preparation

Although this activity calls for a soup can, any can will do. It should be clean because you will be putting your mouth on the can. Punch a hole about 1/8 inch from the bottom of the can with the large nail. You should make sure that there are no rough places around the hole in the can. You don't want to cut your lip. Bleeding distracts too much from the science impact of the demonstration.

Cut the balloon in half and pull the neckless half over the open end of the soup can. Secure it in place with the rubber band. It will look a little like a tiny drum, but it won't sound much like a tiny drum.

Activity

Suck air out of the can and the balloon membrane will be pushed into the can. Blow air into the can and the balloon expands. Suck air out of the can and hold your finger over the hole. Let air into the can a little at a time and the balloon will come out of the can gradually. Blow air into the can and hold your finger over the hole. Let air come out of the can gradually and the balloon will deflate slowly.

Science Concepts and Principles

Sucking air out of the can reduces the air pressure inside the can. The greater air pressure outside the can forces the balloon into the can. Uncovering the hole equalizes the pressure and allows the balloon to return to its original position. This demonstration of air pressure is similar to what happens when you suck pop through a straw. As you suck on the straw you make a partial vaccuum. The greater air pressure on the surface of the pop pushes the pop up the straw into your mouth.

Canned Hot Air

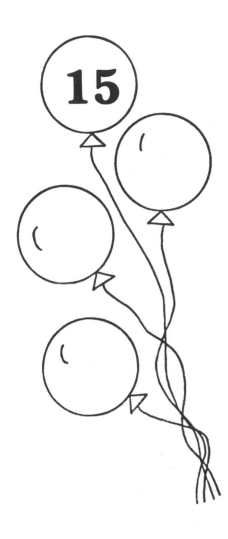

Materials

Can with small mouth

Balloon, 7-inch

Electric toaster

Preparation

Find an appropriate can and clean it out thoroughly. Look for a paint thinner can, brake fluid can, ditto fluid can, or some other can with a screw cap opening. If the can previously contained a volatile material, wash it out thoroughly with detergent.

Activity

Stretch the mouth of the balloon over the mouth of the can. Place the can on a toaster. Turn the toaster on and watch the balloon inflate.

Science Concepts and Principles

Heated air expands if its container allows it. Heating increases the speed of the molecules. This results in greater pressure exerted on the inside of the balloon and it will expand to allow the air inside it to expand.

The Puffing Jug

Materials

Large glass juice jug or 1-liter pop bottle (chilled)

Balloon, 7-inch

Preparation

Put the jug in the refrigerator for at least an hour before you perform this activity.

Activity

Take the jug from the refrigerator. Quickly place the mouth of the balloon over the mouth of the jug. Watch the balloon inflate.

Science Concepts and Principles

As air warms from refrigerator temperature to room temperature, it expands. The balloon inflates to accommodate the increased volume of air.

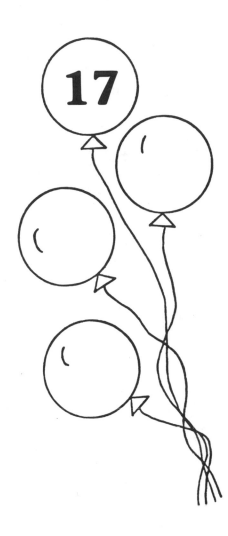

The Uplifting Experience

Materials

Balloon, 7-inch to 9-inch

Book, the heavier the better

Preparation

No advanced preparation is necessary.

Activity

Lay the large deflated balloon near the edge of a table and place a book on top of it. Inflate the balloon and the book will rise.

Science Concepts and Principles

This looks like a dumb activity, but the principle that is demonstrated is extremely important. The air blown into the balloon exerts pressure. Let's say for the sake of argument that the book weighs 5 pounds. If you inflate the balloon with 0.2 pounds per square inch of pressure (an easy feat to accomplish), and the balloon is making 25 square inches of contact with the book, the book will be supported. A 5-pound book can be lifted with 0.2 pounds per square inch of pressure.

There is a price for this easy lift. You will notice that lifting the book this way takes more breath than simply inflating the balloon. To lift the book you must blow into the balloon with enough pressure to inflate *and* lift the book. You must overcome two forces. First, you must overcome the resistive force of the balloon membrane. Second, you must overcome the force of gravity acting on the book.

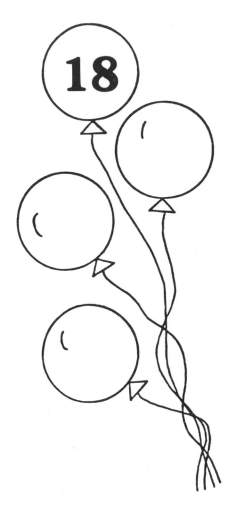

The Second Uplifting Experience

Materials

Freezer zip bag, 1-gallon
Plastic soda straw
Heavy book

Tools

Scissors
Pencil

Preparation

Cut the plastic straw at an angle so that the end is very sharp, like a hypodermic needle. Use the point of the pencil to punch a tiny hole in the plastic bag just below where the bag seals. Push the straw through the hole about an inch inside the bag. Seal the bag. You now have a gasbag that is a little like a balloon but without the elasticity of a balloon. Blow it up by blowing through the straw! If you make the hole small enough and carefully insert the straw, you have an airtight seal around the straw. Notice how much easier the plastic bag is to inflate than a balloon.

Activity

Place the plastic bag near the edge of a table. Place the book on top of the bag. Inflate the bag by blowing through the straw and the book will rise.

Science Concepts and Principles

Unlike the activity titled "The Uplifting Experience," you have only one force to overcome to lift the book. The plastic bag is not elastic like the balloon, so you don't have to overcome elasticity to inflate the bag. When you blow into the bag you produce a pressure that exerts a force on the book. That force is divided over a relatively large surface area so that the book lifts more easily, you will discover, than if you use the balloon.

20

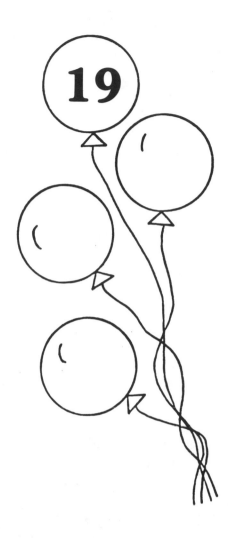

Balloon Cushion

Materials

Large balloon

Chair

Preparation

No advanced preparation required.

Activity

Blow up a balloon to about one half of its capacity, tie off the end, and place the balloon in a chair. Invite a volunteer to sit on the balloon. Normally, the balloon will not burst. You may want to be somewhat judicious in the selection of a volunteer and ask him or her to sit carefully.

Science Concepts and Principles

The air in the balloon exerts a force distributed over a relatively large area so that not too much force is exerted on any one place. Balloons can take a certain amount of force per unit area before they rupture. If you were to have the volunteer sit on a soda can on the balloon, would the balloon pop? Probably, because the weight (force) of the volunteer is exerted over a relatively small area (the area of the top of the soda can). This much force concentrated in a small area will probably cause the balloon to pop.

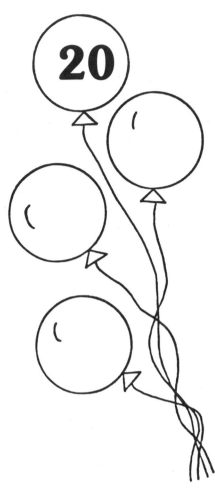

Balloon Megalift

Materials

Balloons, 7-inch to 9-inch (8)

Tables (for example, folding tables) of the same dimension

Preparation

No advanced preparation is required.

Activity

This is a good group activity. Have eight people blow up the balloons until they are roughly the same size, then tie off the ends. Place the balloons uniformly on the top of one of the tables. Turn the second table upside down and place it carefully on top of the balloons on the first table. Surprisingly, the balloons will not burst.

Now, ask for a volunteer to climb up on top of the inverted table. **CAREFUL!** Have people stationed at each leg of the inverted table so that the table will not slide around. Also, caution people about not putting their fingers between the tables. Surprisingly, people's fingers do not support tables as well as balloons. Try to see how many people you can get on top of the table before the balloons pop. Try to keep the weight evenly distributed. **CAREFUL! CAREFUL! CAREFUL!** with this activity.

Science Concepts and Principles

The pressure inside the balloons exerts a force on the surface of the inverted table. That force is distributed over a very large area (the sum of the contacting areas of the eight balloons) so that a relatively large weight can be accommodated.

This activity illustrates the same principle as the famous lying-on-a-bed-of-nails stunt. Suppose a person weighed 100 pounds. If the person sat on one nail, the nail would push back with a force of 100 pounds. If the point of the nail is 1/10th of a square inch, that's 1000 pounds per square inch. Ouch! If the person lays on two nails, the pressure would be 500 pounds per square inch per nail, still enough, no doubt, to cause injury and pain. If, however, the person lays on a bed of 2000 nails then the pressure exerted by each nail would be only ½ pound per square inch, probably not enough to cause a puncture. **However, I wouldn't try this at home**.

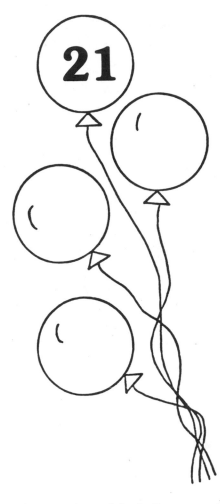

Son of Balloon Megalift

21

Materials

Balloons, 7-inch to 9-inch

Tables of approximately the same dimensions (2)

Preparation

No advanced preparation is required.

Activity

This is a good group activity. Place eight uninflated balloons around the edge of one of the tables with the balloon necks over the edge of the table. Carefully place the second table upside down on top of the balloons on the first table. Next, have eight volunteers gather around the table, one at each balloon. On a signal, all volunteers blow into their balloons at the same time to see if they can lift the table. CAREFUL! Keep fingers, lips, and other parts of anatomies away from the tables. What happens? Nothing. Disappointing, perhaps, but illustrative of a concept.

Science Concepts and Principles

The table is not lifted up by blowing into the balloons because of the nature of balloons. Balloons will inflate at the least resistant point. The table is heavy, so wherever the balloons are in contact with the tables, they encounter resistance. The least resistant point in the balloon is the neck of the balloon when the rest of the balloon is lodged between two very heavy tables. So, the neck of the balloon expands and the rest of the balloon does not.

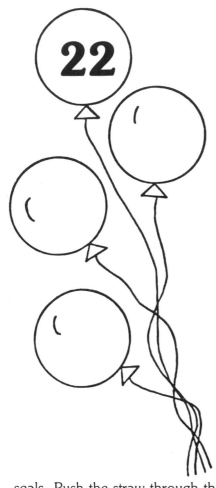

22 Son of Balloon Megalift: A Success Story

Materials

Freezer zip bags, 1-quart (8)

Tables of approximately the same dimensions (2)

Plastic soda straws (8)

Tools

Scissors

Preparation

Cut the plastic straws at an angle so that the ends are very sharp, like a hypodermic needle. Using the point of the scissors, punch a tiny hole in each of the plastic bags just below where the bag seals. Push the straw through the hole about an inch inside the bag. Seal the bag. You now have a gasbag that is like a balloon but lacks elasticity.

Activity

Evenly place the eight gasbags around the edge of the first tabletop, with the edges of the bags and the straws overhanging. Carefully place the second table upside down on top of the first table, which will position the bags between the two tables. Ask for eight volunteers to operate the plastic gasbags, one per bag. On a signal, ask the volunteers to blow into their bags. **CAREFUL!** Keep fingers away from the tables. The table will be lifted by the inflated bags. Now repeat the activity with a volunteer sitting on the table. Be brave—get a weighty volunteer up there. You can do it. **Remember to use spotters for safety**.

Science Concepts and Principles

Unlike activity 21, "Son of Balloon Megalift," there is no point-of-least-resistance problem. All of the air blown into the gasbags is used to lift the table. The surface area over which the sum of the individual forces is exerted is quite large, allowing a few people to lift a relatively heavy table and rider with their breaths.

Chemical Reactions

CONCEPT OF CHEMICAL REACTIONS

When two or more materials are mixed together, and change is observed, we call that change a chemical reaction. The products that result from a chemical reaction are different than those that go into the reaction.

Chemical reactions occur around us every day. Household bleach reacts chemically with soiled fabrics to whiten the materials. Chemical reactions allow automobiles to run. Chemical reactions aid in the digestion of our food and are responsible for the releasing of energy for our bodies. Chemical reactions resulting from "acid rain" cause rapid weathering of stone and metal buildings. One familiar change resulting from a chemical reaction is the conversion of iron to rust.

Many chemical reactions give off a gas as one of the products. Balloons are excellent pieces of equipment for investigating these gassy outcomes because they inflate to reveal the volume of gas released in the reaction.

The words "chemical reaction" have a bad connotation for many people because they think that chemical reactions are necessarily dangerous, involving explosions, vile gases, and toxic products. But this is certainly not always the case. This chapter describes several chemical reactions that are completely safe. And you won't need a lot of fancy show-off laboratory glassware with important-sounding names like beakers, flasks, and test tubes. As you have probably guessed, the reaction vessel of choice in this series of activities is the balloon.

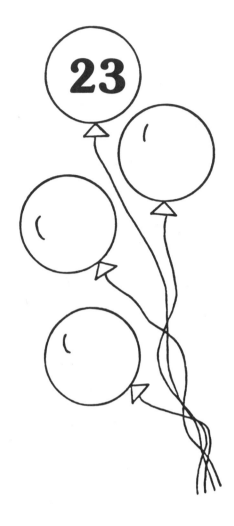

The Old Self-Inflating Balloon Stunt

23

Materials

Balloon, 9-inch

Tablespoon of baking soda

Vinegar, ½ cup

Pop bottle

Preparation

This is a classic demonstration using a balloon. You need to try this ahead of time by yourself before you demonstrate it for someone else. Also, you need to be careful handling the vinegar and baking soda so that they do not mix prematurely, thereby spoiling the surprise of what happens when they mix in the pop bottle. There is a great temptation, once you have performed this activity, to do a little experimentation. You might think that if a little bit of the vinegar and baking soda produce a lot of fun, then a lot of vinegar and soda would produce a lot more fun. There is a point at which, however, that the more fun turns into more mess than you are likely to want to deal with. If the reaction is too large, the balloon will not be able to contain it and it may fly off of the bottle. Be judicious in your experimentation. Use the prescribed amounts of soda and vinegar first, then make slight adjustments if you wish.

Activity

Put 1 tablespoon of baking soda in the balloon. Pour ½ cup of vinegar into the bottle. Place the mouth of the balloon over the neck of the bottle and then lift and shake the balloon so that the baking soda falls into the vinegar. Watch the balloon inflate.

Science Concepts and Principles

There is a chemical reaction between the acetic acid in vinegar and baking soda, which is sodium bicarbonate. One product is a gas, carbon dioxide, which inflates the balloon.

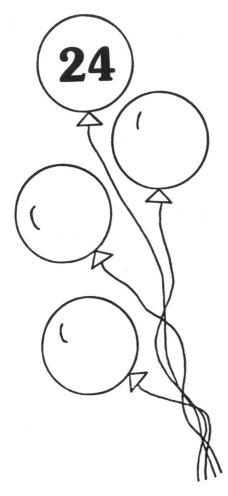

The Other Self-Inflating Balloon Trick

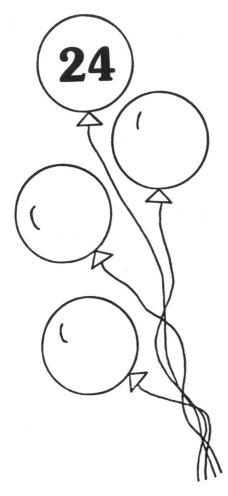

Materials

Balloon, 7-inch

Alka-Seltzer tablets (2)

Water

Tools

Tablespoon

Preparation

You will want to use fresh seltzer tablets—they tend to lose their vitality as they age. Try this by yourself before you demonstrate to others so you will know what to expect. A combination of weak (old) seltzer tablets and a strong balloon can make for very disappointing results.

Activity

Crumble two Alka-Seltzer tablets into a balloon. Add 1 tablespoon of water. Pinch the neck of the balloon and watch the balloon inflate.

Science Concepts and Principles

A chemical reaction between water and the seltzer tablets produces a gas, carbon dioxide, which expands the balloon.

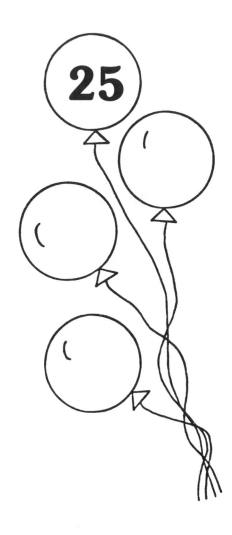

Reversible Balloon

Materials

Balloon, 7-inch

Small-necked glass jar

Steel wool, small wad

Vinegar, 1 teaspoon

Water

Preparation

This is a SLOW activity. It's a lot like the excitement of watching paint peel or an iron nail rust, so don't expect the whiz-bang, rip-snorting results you get from all the other activities in this book. This activity tests your patience. But if you are patient, you can observe some direct evidence of an important chemical reaction.

Activity

Moisten a small pad of steel wool (about the size of a walnut) with a few drops of water and put into the glass jar. Fit an uninflated balloon over the mouth of the jar. Set aside for a few hours and notice that the balloon begins to invert into the jar.

Science Concepts and Principles

A chemical reaction occurs in this activity. The oxygen in the air combines with iron (the steel wool) to produce iron oxide (rust). Because some of the oxygen in the air was removed in the process, a partial vacuum is created. Air pressure outside the jar pushes the balloon into the jar, a region of less air pressure. Other evidence of a chemical reaction can be seen in the changes in the steel wool. It will turn a color very reminiscent of rust. **IT IS RUST!** In this instance, the oxidation (the chemical reaction that produces the rust) occurs very slowly. Sometimes oxidation is a faster and more dramatic process (burning, for example).

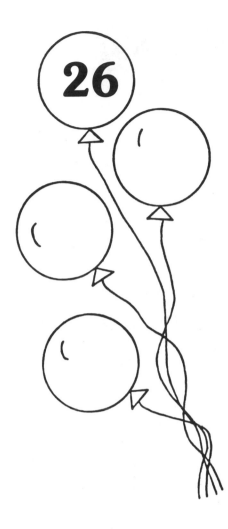

Mmmm, Mmmmm, Good!

26

Materials

Balloon, 5-inch to 7-inch

Glass pop bottle, 6-ounce to 10-ounce

Package of dry yeast, ¼-ounce

Package of dry, sugar-sweetened gelatin dessert (e.g., Jello)

Warm water, 1 cup

Tools

Thermometer

Preparation

Use water at about 100° to 120°F for this activity. This is another of those activities that requires patience.

Activity

Put yeast, gelatin, and warm water in a pop bottle. Put the uninflated balloon over the mouth of the bottle. Watch the balloon SLOWLY expand. This can take a half-hour or so, depending on the freshness of the yeast and temperature of the water.

Science Concepts and Principles

The reaction observed in this activity is actually a complex biochemical reaction in which yeast, a tiny micro-organism, feeds on the sugar in the gelatin. A by-product of the metabolism of yeast is carbon dioxide. It's the yeast metabolism that produces the carbon dioxide that causes bread to rise in preparation for baking. But this is not baking. In fact, the whole thing can smell pretty bad. So, if you enjoy the noxious smells of chemistry you may really groove on this one.

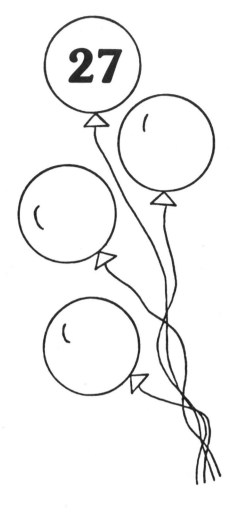

The Air We Breathe

27

Materials

Plastic zip bags (2, gallon size)

Soda straws (2)

Glasses of limewater (2)

Tools

Scissors

Preparation

Put about one tablespoon of lime (not the fruit, but calcium oxide) in each of two six-ounce to eight-ounce glasses of water. Stir it up and you have limewater. If the resulting limewater is milky you will need to filter it. Do this by folding a section of paper towel into fourths, then opening one of the flaps to make a crude funnel. Pour the limewater into that towel funnel and catch the clear liquid in a glass. This clear liquid is still limewater, but is colorless, a property we need to make this demonstration effective. Make gasbags from the gallon-size plastic zip bags by inserting sharpened soda straws as described in activity 18 on page 20.

Activity

Inflate one of the bags by simply opening it wide and sealing the trapped air inside. Submerge the straw in a glass of limewater and gently squeeze the bag so that the air bubbles through the limewater. Observe whether there is a reaction. Evidence of a reaction here will be a change in the color of the limewater. Inflate the second bag by blowing it up through the straw with your breath. Bubble this air through the second glass of limewater and look for evidence of a reaction. The evidence you are looking for is a "milky" white precipitate.

Science Concepts and Principles

The breath contains, among other gases, a relatively high concentration of carbon dioxide, which reacts with the limewater forming a white precipitate, calcium carbonate. Air from the room does not contain the larger quantity of carbon dioxide that the exhaled breath does, therefore, it does not react with the limewater. This demonstration offers some proof of the fact that carbon dioxide is produced in the human respiration process.

Density

CONCEPT OF DENSITY

One of the physical properties of all substances is density. Density is defined as mass per unit volume. Density can be measured in a variety of units, e.g., grams per cubic centimeter, ounces per cubic inch, pounds per cubic foot.

Whether a material floats or sinks in a fluid depends on the relative densities of the two materials. Lead is denser than water. When you cast a lead sinker into a pond it sinks and you fish on the bottom. Cork is less dense than water. When you cast a cork into the pond it floats, and you fish on the surface.

Density of materials sometimes depends on the physical state of the material. Water is H_2O whether it is in a liquid or solid state (ice); however, the density of liquid water is not the same as the density of ice. Ice floats in water so it must be less dense than water. In fact, ice floats with about 90 percent of its mass under water, leaving about 10 percent of its mass poking above the surface. The density of ice is about 0.9 grams per cubic centimeter. The expression, "tip of the iceberg," refers to the smaller part of the iceberg that is visible on the surface of the water.

Specific gravity is used to indicate the relative densities of various substances when compared to liquid water. Water (liquid state) has a specific gravity of 1.0. Ice has a specific gravity of 0.9. Mercury, a very dense metal, has a specific gravity of 13.6. That's a way of saying that mercury has a density 13.6 times greater than water.

Children are sometimes disappointed when the balloon that they blow up does not float high in the air. It's easy to explain. The density of the balloon plus contents (hot air under some pressure) are greater than the density of the air surrounding it. To make a balloon float in air, you need to fill it with a gas less dense than air and enough of it to lift the weight of the balloon. Helium works very nicely if you want a balloon to float in air because the density of helium is about one-seventh the density of air.

Hot-air passenger balloons work because the air inside the balloon bag is very hot and hence, less dense than the air in which it flies. The air in hot-air balloons is heated by a large propane heater. Hot-air balloon travel is most successful early in the morning when the air is generally cooler than it will be the rest of the day. The cool surrounding air is dense compared with the hot air inside the balloon, therefore, maximum lift occurs. There are, of course, some limits to the lifting power of hot-air balloons. Elephants are rarely seen as passengers on these balloons.

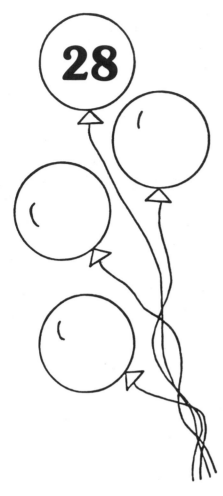

Float or Sink Balloons

Materials

Balloons (2)
Basin or tub
Hot water
Cold water

Preparation

Your only preparation is to find a container large enough to float the balloons. A large plastic tub will do nicely if you don't fill the balloons too full of water.

Activity

Partially fill one balloon with water from the hot tap and another balloon from the cold tap. Place both in a basin or tub containing water at room temperature. The balloon filled with warm water floats; the one filled with cold water sinks.

Science Concepts and Principles

Whether something floats or sinks in a fluid depends on the density of the object relative to the fluid in which it is placed. Warm water is less dense than the water at room temperature and so the balloon filled with warm water floats. Cold water is denser than the water at room temperature and sinks; therefore, the balloon filled with cold water sinks.

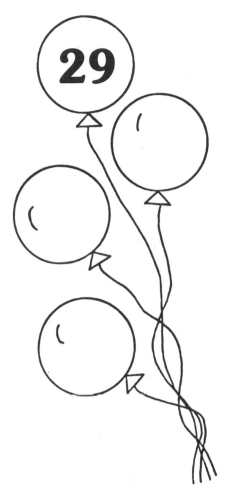

The Cartesian Diver

Materials

Balloon, 9-inch
Narrow-mouth jar or bottle
Rubber band
Medicine dropper

Tools

Scissors

Preparation

Use scissors to cut off the end of a balloon so that the part that you cut off will easily stretch over the mouth of the jar or bottle, forming a taut top. Fill the bottle nearly full of water. Squeeze the bulb on the medicine dropper and fill it with water. Adjust the amount of water in the dropper until it barely floats in the water in the bottle. When properly filled, the dropper will float with just the tip of the rubber bulb above the surface of the water in the bottle. Top off the bottle of water so that it is completely full. Tightly place the tip of the balloon that you cut over the bottle mouth and secure it with the rubber band. Your system is now ready to go.

Activity

You have the "diver" (water-filled medicine dropper) in the water in the bottle and the bottle tautly covered by a piece of balloon secured to the top. Press on the balloon and watch the medicine dropper "dive." Reduce the pressure on the balloon and watch the diver rise. You can put just enough pressure on the balloon to make the medicine dropper stay at whatever level you wish.

Science Concepts and Principles

The balloon acts as a diaphragm. Pressing on the balloon increases pressure. This increased pressure is transmitted throughout water in the bottle in all directions, including the stem of the medicine dropper. The additional pressure on the medicine dropper compresses the air in the stem of the medicine dropper allowing more water to enter the dropper. The density of the dropper is thereby increased so that it becomes denser than water. Denser objects sink in less dense liquids, so the dropper sinks. As you reduce pressure on the balloon diaphragm, the opposite happens. Pressure is reduced in the stem of the dropper and some water in the dropper is expelled. The density of the dropper becomes less and the dropper floats.

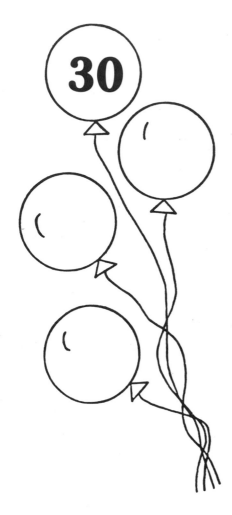

Hot-Air Balloon

Materials

Top ½-inch cut from a margarine tub or similar plastic container
Piece of string, 6-inch
Ultra-thin plastic dry cleaning bag (dress length works best)
Cellophane tape
Hair blow dryer
Cardboard shoe box with lid
Plastic tumbler, 12-ounce to 16-ounce

Preparation

What can be more exciting than a hot-air balloon? This activity enables you to make a small model hot-air balloon and demonstrate the principles of ballooning. CAREFUL! Don't get burned on the hair dryer. Some of these appliances can get very hot. Also, don't let the plastic bag get too close to the dryer or the thin plastic may melt.

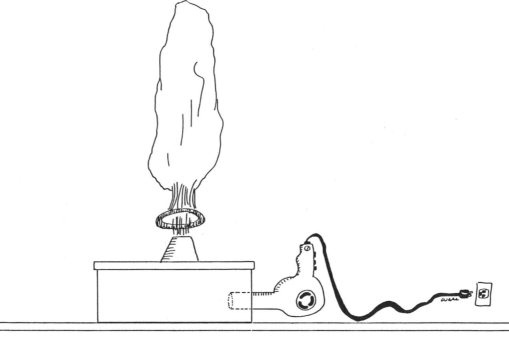

Cut the top ½ inch from the plastic margarine tub. This will serve as the mouth of your hot-air balloon. Carefully, gather in the open end of the plastic garment bag and attach it to the plastic ring with cellophane tape. Plug any holes in the bag with a small amount of tape. Remember, you are trying to keep to a minimum the overall weight of the system.

You also need to construct a hot-air injection system so that you can inflate the plastic bag without melting the plastic. The cardboard shoe box will do nicely for this. Cut a hole the diameter of your hair dryer barrel in the end of the shoe box. Cut a hole slightly smaller than the diameter of the large end of the plastic tumbler in the top of the shoe box. Cut the bottom off of the plastic tumbler. Attach with tape the tumbler, large end down, to the top of the shoe box. Tape on the lid of the shoe box. Now you have your injection system.

With your balloon, injection system, and blow dryer, you are ready to launch!

Activity

Choose a cold, still day for this activity. If you have access to a big old gymnasium early on a winter morning, take advantage of it. Ask a helper or two to hold the plastic bag open and erect over the small end of the tumbler that is attached to the shoe box top. Have another helper hold the injection system (shoe box) in place. Direct the flow of the hair dryer into the hole in the side of the shoe box. This will allow hot air to flow through the small end of the tumbler and into the plastic garment bag. When the balloon fills with hot air, it will rise.

Science Concepts and Principles

The less dense warm air in the balloon rises because the more dense surrounding air pushes it up. The hair dryer heats the air inside the plastic bag, reducing the density of the balloon system, permitting the model balloon to rise. The secret to the success of this hot-air balloon model is that all the flying components must be lightweight because the hot air is only slightly less dense than the cooler air surrounding it.

Floating Balloon

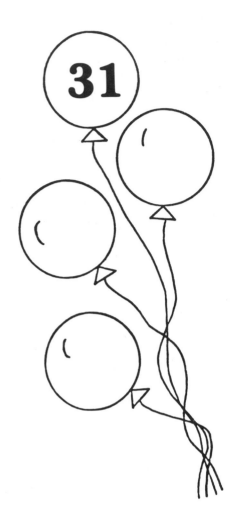

Materials

Balloon, 9-inch

Sink or large container of water

Preparation

No advanced preparation is necessary.

Activity

Inflate the balloon and tie off its end. Ask a friend to completely submerge the balloon. It will be difficult or impossible, depending, of course, on how strong your friend is.

Science Concepts or Principles

The balloon floats in water because it is not nearly as dense as the water. Buoyancy is a tricky concept to think through, but let's see if we can figure it out.

All objects that are placed in a fluid are buoyed up (lifted) by a force equal to the weight of the volume of fluid they displace. If the object is heavier than the volume of fluid it displaces, the object will sink in the fluid. If the object is lighter than the volume of fluid it can displace, it will float.

Consider a block of wood as the object and water as the fluid. If you hold the block under water, the volume of water it displaces is a little heavier than the weight of the block. Therefore it floats. But, if you look closely, you will see that part of the block is under water. In fact, the volume of water displaced by the portion of the block under water will be exactly equal in weight to the block.

Now the balloon…. When we release an air-filled balloon in the air, it sinks because the balloon and air system weighs more than the air it displaces. But when we put it in water, it hardly puts a dent in the surface. The difference between the weight of the balloon and the weight of the water it displaces is tremendous, so it is difficult to submerge the balloon. This principle is used in the design of life rafts. Air-filled rafts float very high in water and can take a considerable load before they sink.

36

Gravity and Momentum

CONCEPT OF GRAVITY

Gravity affects us and the way we live probably more than any other force in the universe. If we slip, we fall. Thanks, gravity! As we grow older, we sag. Thanks, gravity! We can jump only so far and so high, thanks to gravity.

Gravity is the force of attraction that exists between two objects. Every object (body) is attracted to every other object. There is an attraction between the moon and the earth that causes tides. There is an attraction between the sun and the earth that enables the earth to maintain its orbit. There is an attraction between any celestial body and any other body. All bodies attract all other bodies with a force that diminishes as the distance between the bodies increases. We can say that the force of attraction is directly proportional to the mass (amount of matter in a body) and inversely proportional to the square of the distance between the bodies. A measure of the force between the earth and anything on earth is the weight of the object.

Weight measures the amount of mass in a body and the force it exerts on the earth. "Which weighs more, a pound of feathers or a pound of lead?" is a trick question often asked of children. The answer: They weigh the same. But a pound of feathers takes up much more space than a pound of lead. That is a function of their density, a concept we have already discussed in chapter 3.

Air has mass, and, therefore, is controlled by the gravity exerted by the earth. If we fill a balloon with air and tie it off, it will not float. The weight of the balloon and the air inside it are heavier than the air surrounding the balloon, so it will sink. A balloon filled with helium will float in the air. Does this mean that helium is not affected by gravity? No. Helium has mass, although its mass for a given volume (at the same pressure) is less than the mass of a similar volume of air. A helium balloon floats in air because the average density of the helium and the balloon is less than the density of the air surrounding it. If a helium-filled balloon were dropped in a vacuum, a space that had no air or any other substance, then it would fall to the earth.

Several activities in this book are designed to let you observe the force of gravity on various balloon systems. Remember that the effect of gravity on falling objects is not always easy to observe. Wind currents and air resistance often mask the force of gravity.

CONCEPT OF MOMENTUM

An object in motion has a momentum. The greater the velocity of the object, the greater its momentum. That accounts for the fact that tornado-driven pieces of straw have been found sticking right through 6-inch-thick wooden fence posts. And, the greater the mass of the object, the greater the momentum. A multiton tanker traveling at a speed of 1 mile per hour can crush an entire docking facility. Objects with lots of momentum have the ability to move other objects out of their way. Can you imagine the chaos in the wake of a tornado-driven tanker?

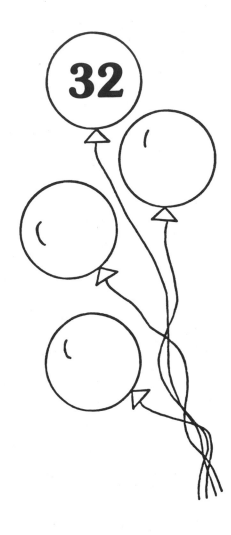

... Like a Lead Balloon

Materials

Balloons, 7-inch (2)

Spray deodorant in an aerosol can

Preparation

No advanced preparation is necessary.

Activity

Blow up one balloon and tie off its end. Hold the mouth of the second balloon over the nozzle of the aerosol can and fill it to the same diameter with gas from the aerosol can and tie off its end. Drop both balloons at the same time and see which one hits the floor first.

Science Concepts and Principles

Different gases have different densities. Gravity acts on the two balloons equally, pulling them to earth with equal force. The balloon filled with the denser gas from the aerosol can has a greater mass. It will fall faster because it is able to plow through the resisting air more effectively. If there were no air to offer resistance they would fall at the same speed.

Gravity Balloons

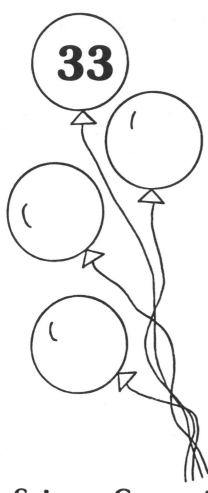

Materials

Balloons, 9-inch to 11-inch (2)

Preparation

No advanced preparation is necessary.

Activity

Inflate one balloon to capacity and the other to about half that size. Tie them off. Drop both balloons at the same time to see which falls faster. Either one might win.

Science Concepts and Principles

The balloons may fall with about the same speed, or the smaller may fall faster. It all depends on a delicate balance between weight and area of the cross section. The larger balloon will be more massive. However, air resistance keeps its speed down. The smaller balloon does not have as much mass, but it does not have to confront as much air resistance due to its smaller size. It's hard to predict which of your balloons will fall faster. Our small one consistently beats the larger one.

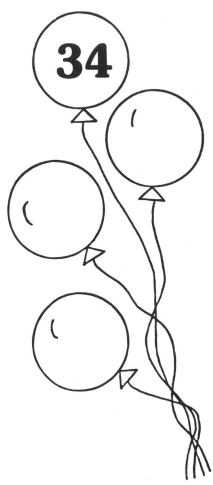

Bouncing Balloons

Materials

Balloons, 9-inch (4)

Preparation

No advanced preparation is necessary.

Activity

Inflate balloons to various sizes and tie off ends. Dribble balloons as you would a basketball. What size balloon is easiest to handle?

Science Concepts and Principles

Balloons will bounce because they are elastic, but they are not as easy to bounce as basketballs. Why? Basketballs are heavier than balloons and are not affected as much by air resistance. Air resistance has very little effect on basketballs as they are dribbled. Balloons are another matter. The smaller mass of the balloons makes them be affected by air resistance. Generally, the smaller balloons, because of their smaller volume and greater average density, are less affected by resistance of air and are slightly easier to handle. However, if you really want to demonstrate your dribbling ability, use a basketball rather than a balloon.

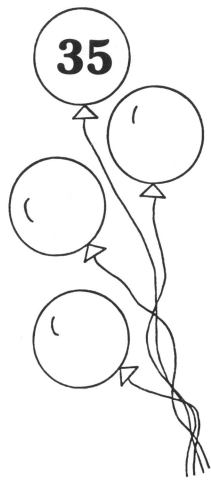

What Goes Up Must Come Down

Materials

Balloons, 7-inch (2)

Pieces string, 10 inches long (2)

Metal washers (2)

Preparation

No advanced preparation is necessary.

Activity

Inflate two balloons to the same size and tie off the ends. Attach a string to each. Attach two washers to one of the strings. Drop the balloons from the same height to see which one falls fastest. The balloon with weight will fall faster.

Science Concepts and Principles

Why will the balloon with weights fall faster? Because the weighted balloon is heavier? Yes. Acceleration due to gravity is a constant in falling bodies. However, the more massive object will accelerate a little longer. The unweighted balloon accelerates for a very short time until its weight is equalled by air resistance. In a vacuum, where air resistance is not a factor, all balloons, irrespective of the number of washers that are along for the ride, fall at the same speed.

Balloon Races

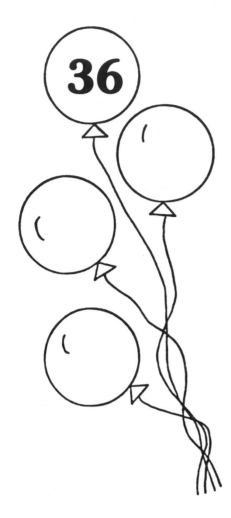

Materials

Balloons (4)

Dried kidney beans (12)

Permanent marking pen

Preparation

Inflate four balloons to the same size and tie off their ends. But before you do, put two beans into one balloon, four into another, six into the third, and none into the fourth. Label the balloons A, B, C, and D, arbitrarily.

Activity

Tell your audience that your balloons are full of beans, but you don't know which is the fullest. (They may think you are full of beans, but carry on anyway.) Challenge them to arrange the balloons in order from heaviest to lightest based on drop races. The balloons with more beans travel fastest.

Science Concepts and Principles

Again, this puzzle can be solved by observing which balloon travels fastest. The balloons with more mass (greater number of beans) accelerate a little longer before they reach a constant speed at which the weight is equal to the air resistance.

Comparing Gases

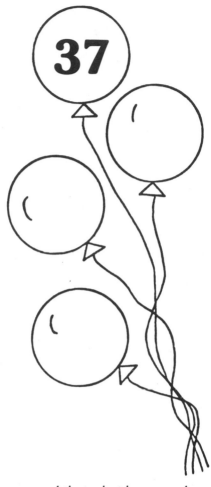

37

Materials

Balloons, 7-inch (2)

Tablespoon of baking soda

Vinegar, about ½ cup

Tall glass pop bottle, 6-ounce to 10-ounce

Bicycle tire pump (optional)

Preparation

No advanced preparation is necessary. However, you should prepare yourself for various results when you do this activity. The balloons are very nearly the same weight and both are susceptible to strange air currents in your room. Don't predict out loud what will happen when you do an activity like this. It's fine to get those who watch to make predictions, but it's usually bad form for you to predict. The main reason is that you'll look bad when your predictions aren't accurate. It's also bad form to say something that begins with "What was supposed to happen was...." Be assured that what happened was supposed to happen. Nature is that way. It doesn't allow something to happen just because you think it should.

Activity

Put the baking soda into the uninflated balloon and the vinegar into the bottle. Carefully place the mouth of the balloon over the bottle top and then tip the baking soda into the bottle. When the balloon inflates, remove and tie off its end. Inflate a second balloon to the same size with air (a bicycle pump is best for this because only air is introduced into the balloon) and tie off its end. See which one falls faster when both are dropped from the same height.

Science Concept and Principles

Carbon dioxide is produced in the chemical reaction between the baking soda and vinegar, and is denser than air. So, the heavier carbon dioxide balloon accelerates a little longer until it reaches a constant speed at which the weight of the balloon is equal to the air resistance. **Caution:** Choose a bottle tall enough so that the foam from the reaction does not enter the balloon. The extra weight contributed by the foam can cause some astute onlookers to question the validity of your results.

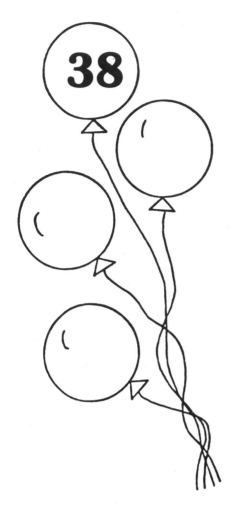

Blowing in the Wind

Materials

Balloons, 7-inch (6)

Preparation

No advanced preparation is necessary.

Activity

Inflate the balloons to varying sizes and tie off the ends. Release them outside in the wind to see how far each goes and how each is affected by the wind. Do all balloons act the same regardless of the size?

Science Concepts and Principles

The size of each balloon determines how that balloon is affected by air resistance. The larger balloons will usually be more erratic in their movement because their larger cross section makes them more susceptible to the vagaries of wind currents.

Note: Be sure to track down and retrieve all of the balloons. Balloons are fun and educational, as we are sure you have realized by now, but they are no good in the environment.

Membranes

CONCEPT OF MEMBRANES

One of the wonderful things about balloons is the very stuff from which they are made—a stretchable, semipermeable membrane. Actually, the balloon fabric is an artificial membrane; scientifically speaking (we do that sometimes), a membrane stems from organic sources. Membranes with which you may have some familiarity are the critically important cell membranes that surround each and every living cell, providing a variety of filtering and regulating functions, and mucous membranes that line our noses and throats. But this is of little interest to us in this book because it is a well accepted scientific fact that cell membranes and mucous membranes make lousy balloons.

Balloons are neat because the fabric is tough, has good memory (returns to its original shape), expands tremendously and fairly uniformly, can be made quite transparent, and is semipermeable. This last characteristic means that some kinds of materials (molecules) can pass right through the walls of the balloon but others cannot. And perhaps best of all, balloons are cheap. In fact, pound for pound balloons may be the best bargain in science education. And, let's face it, a balloon is probably the only piece of scientific apparatus that is synonymous with a good time. Let's promote the balloon as the symbol for safe science.

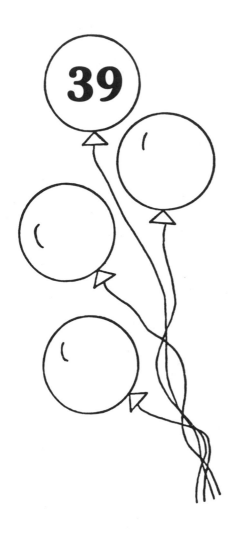

A Growing Line

Materials

Balloon, 7-inch
Felt tip pen (black is best)

Tools

Ruler
Measuring tape

Activity

Draw a line 1 inch long on an uninflated balloon. Inflate the balloon and measure the length of the line. Try to determine the relationship between the circumference of the balloon and the length of the line. You can make a table like the one below to help you see if there is a relationship.

Circumference of Balloon	Length of Line

How good can you become as a predictor? Make a graph from the data in your chart and see if that helps you make predictions. Does it make a difference on what part of the balloon the line is drawn? Does the balloon stretch thinner in some parts than others? Does this affect the length of the line?

Science Concepts and Principles

Balloons are stretchable. Every feature on their surface expands when the balloon is expanded. The lines on the balloon expand in certain predictable patterns depending on where they're drawn. Balloons stretch more in the middle than on the ends. The rubber is thinner in these areas of the balloons. Not surprisingly, it turns out that the greatest stretching of the line occurs in the areas most stretched.

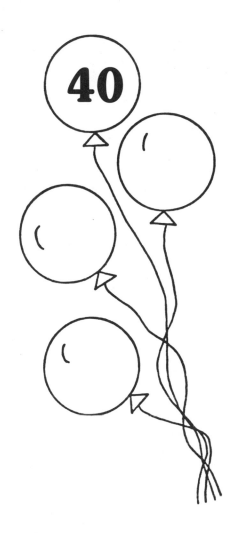

How Did the Letters Grow?

Materials

Balloon, 7-inch

Felt marker (black is best)

Tools

Ruler

Preparation

No advanced preparation is necessary.

Activity

Write your name or a word on a balloon in very small letters. Measure the height of the letters. Inflate the balloon and watch the size of the letters change. Measure the height of the letters on the inflated balloon. How many times larger did the letters get? Can you predict how big to blow the balloon to make the letters twice as high as on the uninflated balloon? Three times? Four times? Ten times? How does a circle or square look after expansion?

Science Concepts and Principles

The balloon is stretchable. The inflated balloon is thinner than the uninflated balloon, the material in the balloon being spread over a larger area. The area on which the word is written expands making the word larger.

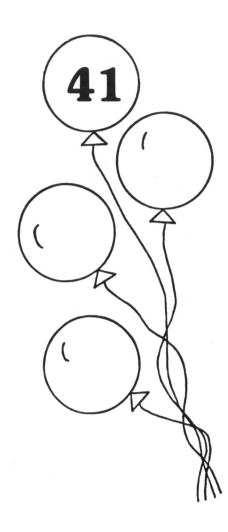

Our Expanding Universe

Materials

Balloon, 12-inch
Felt marker (black is best)
Cloth measuring tape

Preparation

No advanced preparation is necessary.

Activity

Blow up the balloon halfway. Pinch off the neck of the balloon. Make a dot on the balloon and place a zero beside it indicating "origin." Mark four or five other dots in a straight line three inches apart and designate with the letters "A," "B," "C," etc. Continue inflating the balloon and measuring the distances to the other dots. (Those farther away have moved a greater distance.) You can record the results in a table like this one.

Dot	A	B	C	D	E	F
Starting Distance from the origin						
Final Distance from the origin						

Science Concepts and Principles

The balloon expands when inflated. All areas of the balloon expand, but not equally. This activity provides a model of our expanding universe. You can suppose that the original dot was where it all started. The other dots can be galaxies distancing themselves from the origin. And if you continue to explore this model of the ever-expanding universe, eventually you will come full circle and experience once again the "big bang." I guarantee it!

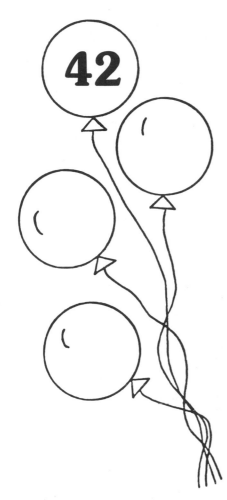

Air Has Mass

Materials

Balloons, 7-inch (2)

Soda straws (2)

Paper clips (2, same size)

Thread

Pin

Preparation

Stick one straw a short distance inside another to make a long straw beam. Make hooks out of the paper clips and run one through each end of the straw beam (see illustration). Hang a length of thread from the ceiling or other high structure and tie the free end to the center of the straw beam.

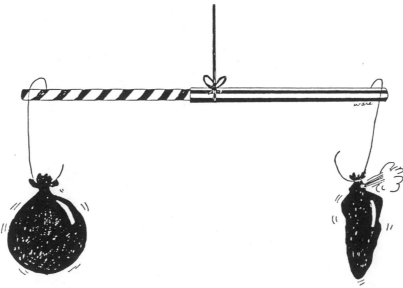

(Activity continued on page 50.)

Activity

Blow up two balloons to the same size and tie them off. Attach one to each end of the beam. Carefully balance the system by moving the fulcrum (thread) to and fro. When the students agree that the system is balanced, ask what they think will happen when the air is let out of one of the balloons. Let the air out of one balloon.

Note: Popping the balloon is dramatic, but part of the balloon can be lost in the process. Air can be let out in a controlled manner by piercing the rubber with a pin right near the knot.

Ask the students to explain why the inflated balloon is heavier than the deflated one. Ask the students what they think would happen if they were to hang two water balloons on a balance beam under water and then pop one. Would the balloon still filled with water go down?

Science Concepts and Principles

Air is real stuff—matter. Like all matter, air occupies space and has mass. Because we live in an environment where air already fills every space where it is allowed to flow, we can't simply put air into a container and weigh it on a balance as we would most other materials. Nor can we use plastic bags to verify that air has mass. If one balances two sealed zip bags filled with air and then squeezes all the air out of one, they will still balance. But balloons can demonstrate that air has mass because the pressure exerted by the rubber membrane compresses the air in the balloon. There is actually more air in a balloon than there is in a comparable space outside the balloon. A greater amount of air is heavier than a smaller amount of air, so air must have mass.

No, the water balloon stunt won't work. Liquids are not compressible, so the water in a balloon weighs exactly the same as an equal volume outside the balloon. Result: no imbalance.

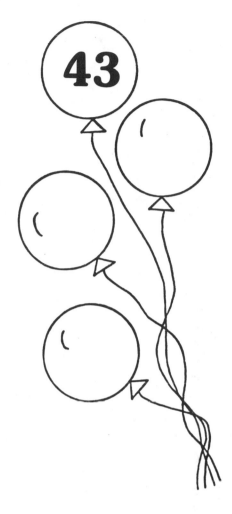

Two Balloons in One

Materials

Balloons, 7-inch (two per student volunteer)

Preparation

No advanced preparation is necessary. This is a good inquiry-building activity. There are quite a few ways to inflate one balloon inside another but each way takes thought. Basically, you have to place one uninflated balloon inside another to begin. Inflate the inside balloon to a relatively small diameter, tie off its end, and push it as far inside as you can. Next, inflate the outside balloon and tie it off.

Activity

Call for a volunteer, hand him or her two balloons and ask that he or she inflate one balloon inside another. Call for other onlookers to make suggestions and call on additional volunteers to see if they can do it; particularly, if they can do it in a different way.

Science Concepts and Principles

Several strategies will need to be explored before a technique is discovered to overcome the problems of this request. Remember that two objects cannot occupy the same space at the same time. It takes some thought to determine how the space is to be shared.

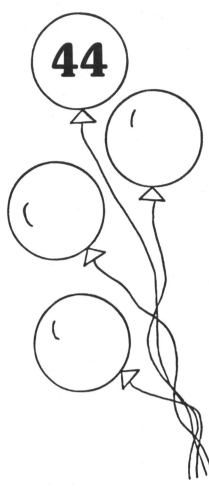

The Discrepant Event

Materials

Balloons, 9-inch (2)
Plastic film canisters, 35-mm (2)
Aquarium hose, about 8 inches
Aquarium hose tee or wye
Alligator clips (2)

Tools

Scissors
Needle-nose pliers
Drill (about 3/16-inch) or pointed knife

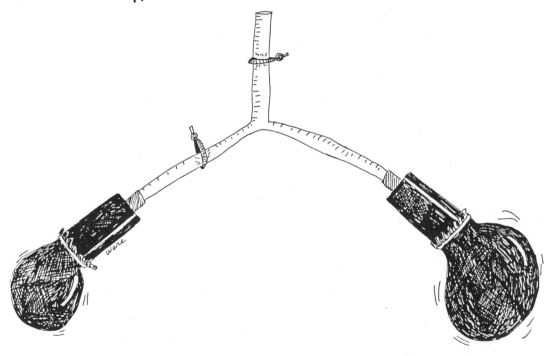

Preparation

This demonstration takes a little extra preparation, but it is worth it. Drill a hole in the center of the bottom of the two plastic film canisters. Cut the hose into three equal parts and shove one section on each end of the tee. Cut at a sharp angle the ends of the two hose sections that are on the two ends of the cross bar of the tee. They should look like the tips of huge hypodermic needles. Poke the point of one hose through the hole in the bottom of one canister and use the needle-nose pliers to pull about ½ inch of hose through the hole. It should be a TIGHT fit—in fact, airtight. Do the same thing with the other canister. Pull a balloon over the mouth of each canister and have the clips handy. Ready!

Activity

Blow through the open end of the hose. One balloon will inflate. When it is about 5 inches in diameter place a clip on the hose between the inflated balloon and the tee. Continue to blow and watch the second balloon inflate until it is about 7 inches in diameter. Place a clip on the inflator hose.

Ask the observers what they think will happen when you remove the clip that is preventing air from flowing between the two balloons. Hold the system with the small balloon above the larger one and release the clip that is between the tee and the small balloon.

Science Concepts and Principles

Expandable rubber membranes, like those used to make balloons, exert pressure on their contents. However, the membranes weaken as they are stretched. Therefore, the less-inflated of two identical balloons will exert a stronger force on its contents than the larger balloon. (Think about it. Is it harder to blow up a balloon at first or after it has had a large volume of air inside?)

When you do this demonstration you will discover that the air under greater pressure (smaller balloon) is pushed into the larger balloon until the pressure is equalized—usually when the smaller balloon is reduced to its uninflated size. This is a dandy stunt to get people thinking.

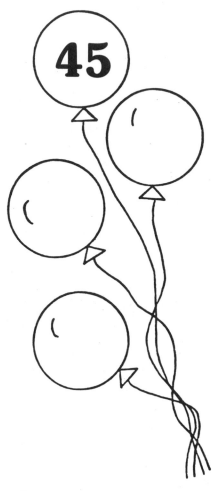

A Piercing Moment

Materials

Balloon, 9-inch

Cellophane tape

Needle

Cotton for ear plugs (optional)

Preparation

No advanced preparation is necessary. This activity takes a steady hand and steady nerves. Many people are terrified at the thought of a bursting balloon. That might happen. Practice, however, will make you more confident. Soon it will be your audience, and not you, who will be terrified.

Activity

Inflate the balloon but not too large. Tie off the end and place a small strip of tape on the surface of the balloon. Pierce the balloon through the tape. It shouldn't pop, but it's always a good idea to steel yourself against that possibility. You can hedge your bets slightly if you choose a place to put the tape where the balloon is not stretched very tightly.

Science Concepts and Principles

Normally, a balloon pops when it is pierced with a needle. The reason for this is that the needle causes the taut balloon membrane to tear suddenly and make the resulting explosion. Rubber and tape have different characteristics. The tape is stronger and won't tear when the needle penetrates the balloon. The tape acts as a reinforcer.

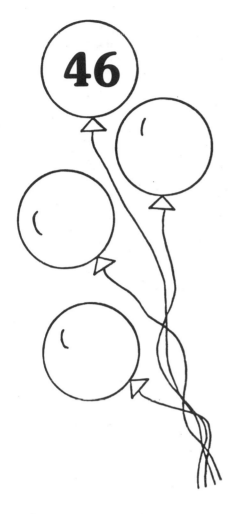

A Piercing Moment: Act II

Materials

Balloon, 9-inch

Long, thin, smooth, sharp, metal knitting needle

Preparation

No advanced preparation is necessary. If you had success with A Piercing Moment, the previous activity, you are ready for the big time! A knitting needle through a balloon? No sweat! Let's put a large needle, a needle that people can actually see into a balloon. Also, we're not going to hedge with the use of cellophane tape. This activity takes steady hands and steady nerves. Practice will make you confident that the balloon won't pop when pierced with this long needle. It helps if the needle is lubricated a bit. Rub the needle through your hair. This normally provides enough oil to properly lubricate the needle. If your hair is not oily or if you are bald, use some petroleum jelly as a lubricant. In a pinch, use the sweat that is by now accumulating in your palm.

Activity

Inflate a balloon until it is pretty large, but don't get it too "tight." Let some air out. Tie off the end. Hold the balloon in one hand and carefully push the needle through the less taut rubber near the mouth of the balloon. Twist the needle as you insert it. If things are going well and you feel confident, continue to insert the needle, aiming it at the tip end (opposite the mouth end) of the balloon where once again the rubber is thicker and less taut. Push the needle through the tip of the balloon so that the balloon is completely skewered. If you do this right, the balloon should not pop.

Science Concepts and Principles

Normally, a balloon pops when it is stuck with a big old needle. The reason for this is that the needle causes the taut balloon membrane to tear suddenly with the familiar exciting explosion. The trick is to insert the needle in an area where the balloon is not so taut, near the knot of the balloon and at the tip where the membrane is always noticeably thicker. The intrusion of the needle is so gradual in these thick areas that the membrane allows the needle to pass through easily, actually pushing the molecules of rubber out of the way. The membrane stretches tightly around the needle as it passes through so that the tiny hole made by the needle is almost "repaired." This is a great demonstration when you can pull it off. This is a lousy demonstration when it fails and the surprising bang causes you to stab yourself with the very sharp knitting needle.

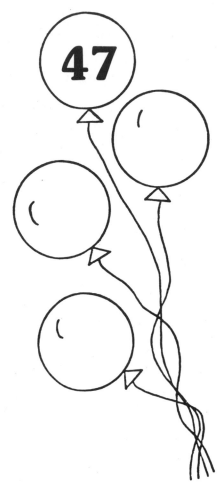

Are Balloons Airtight?

Materials

Balloons, 7-inch, from three different sources, if possible (3)

Measuring tape

Paper and pencil for recording data

Preparation

This is one of those activities that takes so long for the results to come in that it isn't too much fun to watch. If you are into immediate results, there are oodles of activities in this book that provide them. This, however, isn't one of them.

Activity

Inflate and securely tie off three balloons. Measure and record the circumference of each. Make measurements over the next three days (or longer) to see what happens to the size of the balloons. You might use a chart like the one that follows. Is there a relationship between the time and the amount of air lost? If you want to get mathematical and if you have nearly spherical balloons, you can calculate the volume of air in the balloons by the formula:

$$V = \frac{C^3}{60}$$

where

$V =$ volume

$C^3 =$ circumference cubed

Balloon #	1	2	3
Circumference Day 1			
Circumference Day 2			
Circumference Day 3			

Science Concepts and Principles

The rubber membrane used to make most balloons is actually filled with holes—very tiny holes, but holes. Gas molecules can pass through the walls of a typical balloon. It might be interesting to find out which gas molecules escape most readily through balloon membranes. Can you set up an experiment to see if the air inside the balloon is lost at a steady rate? Would air in a balloon escape slower as the pressure inside decreases?

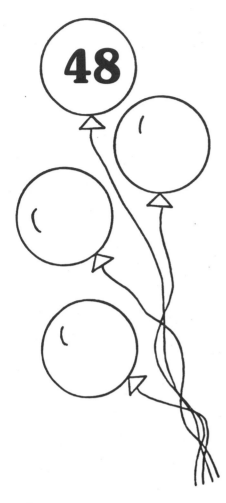

48 *Semipermeable Membranes*

Materials

Balloons (3)

Pungent liquids (3, e.g., cologne, peppermint extract, vanilla extract)

Funnel

Marking pen, permanent

Preparation

Use a funnel to pour a small amount of the three liquids into three separate balloons. Be careful not to spill liquids on the outside of the balloons. Tie a knot in each balloon and label them 1, 2, and 3. Bear in mind that some students are very sensitive, even allergic, to some odors. Don't require close olfactory observations if students express resistance.

Activity

Bring out the mystery balloons. Ask the students to guess what is in each balloon based on their observations. Soon the students should detect the odors coming through the membranes. Ask the students for their ideas to explain why they can smell right through the balloon.

Science Concepts and Principles

Permeable membranes allow all molecules to move freely back and forth from one side to the other. If you put up a sign next to the open door of your house that says, "No flies," flies will come and go as they please, so will dogs, chickens, and neighbors. That is like a permeable membrane. A semipermeable membrane acts as a barrier to some molecules and allows for the passage of others. A chicken wire hen house will keep the chickens in and the fox out, but the flies are still able to move through easily. Chicken wire is impermeable to chickens and foxes, but permeable to flies.

Rubber balloon membranes are permeable to most gases, including those that have strong odors. The molecules of peppermint can pass right through the wall of the balloon and interact with our smelling mechanism to tip us off to what is in the balloon. The membrane is relatively impermeable to water molecules.

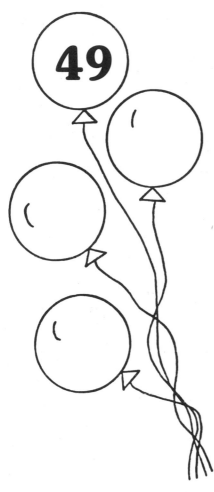

The Spouting Water Balloon

49

Materials

Balloon, 9-inch

Straight pin or sewing needle

Running water

Preparation

No advanced preparation is necessary.

Activity

Pull the mouth of the balloon over the faucet of a water tap and partially fill the balloon with water. Prick a small pinhole on the side of the balloon (just below the neck). Turn the water back on at a slow pace. As the balloon fills, water first squirts farther and farther from the balloon, but then it does a reversal, squirting shorter and shorter distances. Curious behavior! Come to think of it, this is a good activity to do with the hose out in the yard on a nice sunny day. Then it won't matter so much if you get wet.

Science Concepts and Principles

As you would expect, water flows from the hole in the balloon. The distance the water squirts out from the balloon is an indication of the pressure on the water. As the balloon inflates, the hole in the balloon gets larger. This reduces the pressure under which the water escapes. Confused? Consider water running out a garden hose. How do you make the water squirt farther? By covering part of the opening with your finger! Reducing the size of the opening causes the water to escape under greater pressure as evidenced by the greater distance the escaping water travels.

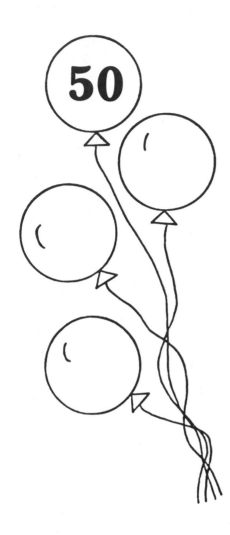

Water Balloon Toss

Materials

Balloon, 9-inch, one for each participant

Water

Bathing suits (optional)

Preparation

Make a batch of water balloons. Arrange for a warm and sunny day, and possibly a picnic atmosphere.

Activity

This is an activity best conducted outdoors. You can improvise all sorts of games, including catch, relay races, and so forth. Pitch balloons gingerly; catch them carefully.

Science Concepts and Principles

O.K. You've got us. There is no great scientific principle illustrated in this activity. This is for sheer fun. If you can't have fun throwing water balloons around, we're sorry. The possibility for disaster heightens the interest in this activity. Who can complete the longest successful toss and catch?

Propulsion

CONCEPT OF PROPULSION

Sir Isaac Newton figured out some basic laws that govern the motion of objects. He observed that objects in motion tend to stay in motion, and objects at rest tend to stay at rest. That's the first law. He went on to determine that if a force is brought to bear on an object, the object will accelerate in the direction the force is acting. Makes sense. That's the second law of motion. And he also observed that if one object exerts a force on a second object, the second object exerts an equal force on the first object, but in the opposite direction. That's Newton's third law of motion, and it is often stated, for every action there is an equal and opposite reaction. So, if you sit in an office chair with the nice well-lubricated wheels and start chucking potatoes down the hall in a southerly direction, you will slowly move north until you run into some kind of barrier.

That's exactly what you can make a balloon do. Fill it up with potatoes (air molecules) under pressure so that it is ready to start pitching them out of the neck of the balloon as soon as it can. Now you have an analogous situation. As the balloon starts to expel air out the neck, it starts to propel itself in the opposite direction. The greater the speed of the expelled air, the greater the speed of the flight.

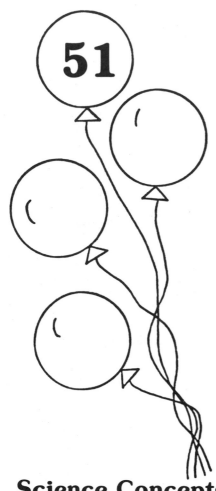

Jet Propulsion

51

Materials

Balloon, long is best

Preparation

No advanced preparation is necessary.

Activity

Inflate balloon and pinch off end. Let go and see how it is propelled.

Science Concepts and Principles

Newton's third law of motion: For every action there is an equal and opposite reaction. The escaping air presents an action. The balloon reacts by being propelled erratically in the opposite direction.

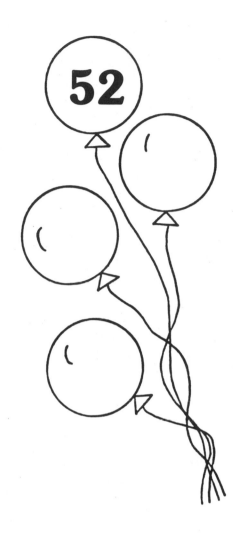

Zoom Balloons

Materials

Balloons—long, skinny ones work best

Preparation

No advanced preparation is necessary.

Activity

Line up students in single file facing one way. Have each student inflate a balloon and see who can make his/her balloon fly the greatest distance. Encourage experimentation to see who can come up with a good guidance system; for example, would fins glued on a balloon help it go straighter?

Science Concepts and Principles

Newton's third law of motion: For each action there is an opposite and equal reaction. The air escaping from the balloon is an action. The balloon being propelled in the opposite direction is evidence of reaction.

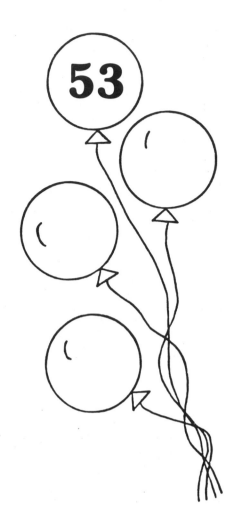

Balloons and Marbles

Materials

Balloon

Glass marble

Preparation

No advanced preparation is necessary.

Activity

Inflate a balloon and release it. Observe its flight characteristics. Now place a marble inside the balloon. Inflate it and release it again. Again, observe its flight characteristics. Compare the two flight paths.

Science Concepts and Principles

Newton's third law of motion: For every action there is an opposite and equal reaction. The action of the air being released causes the reaction of the balloon being propelled. The path of the balloon is less erratic when there is a marble on board because the mass of the marble increases the momentum of the balloon, making the balloon less susceptible to wind anomalies that tend to deflect the path of the balloon.

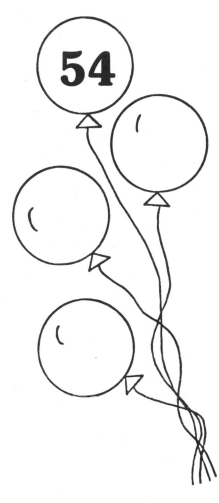

Balloon Time

Materials

Round balloons, one for each four students

Stopwatch or clock with sweep second hand

Preparation

No preparation is required for this activity other than to locate enough round balloons for each four students. Balloons should be the same size.

Activity

This activity is designed to gather information on the relationship between the number of puffs used in inflating a balloon and the length of time a released inflated balloon will stay in the air. Each member of a group of four has a job. One person should be responsible for inflating and releasing the balloon. A second person should be the timer. A third person should be responsible for observing the flight of the balloon and yelling "go" and "stop" to the timer. The fourth person should be the recorder. If a stopwatch is used, the timer will not need a person to yell "go" and "stop."

First, stretch the balloons so that inflation will be more easily accomplished. Next, the designated "puffer" puts two puffs of air into the balloon. The balloon is released and the time it stays in the air is recorded.

Repeat with successively increased numbers of puffs—4, 6, 8, 10, and so forth. A decision needs to be made about a "standard" size of a puff and a standard release technique. The recorder keeps a record of the results on a data sheet that looks like this:

(Activity continues on page 66.)

Number of puffs	Number of seconds in the air
2	1.5
4	2.0
6	3.5
8	4.5
10	5.5
•	•
•	•

Next, make a point-line graph on a grid so that the relationship can be shown in a different way. Students may need help with constructing a graph. The independent variable (number of puffs) goes on the horizontal axis and the dependent variable (time in the air) goes on the vertical axis. Place numbers on both axes with the intersection being "0" on each. The result will be nearly a straight line. Encourage students not to connect the dots but to draw a line that shows the general trend of the relationship.

Science Concepts and Principles

Air in the balloon is under pressure. When the balloon is released the air under pressure rushes out, propelling the balloon and serving as an illustration of Newton's third law of motion. The amount of time the balloon will stay in the air depends on how long the force of air rushing from the balloon will be exerted. That time is dependent on how much air is in the balloon, so the time in the air is roughly proportional to the amount of air in the balloon. Other factors also contribute. The route the balloon takes is random. You can start it off in a vertical position but the path the balloon takes cannot be accurately predicted. It may rise sharply, change directions abruptly, and nose dive into the floor.

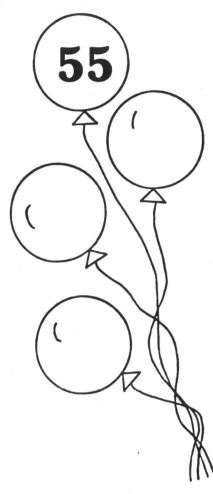

Balloon Rockets

Materials

Balloons, long style

Quart-size plastic bag

Roll of 10 lb. test monofilament fishing line

Soda straw

Cellophane tape

Duct tape

Preparation

Use cellophane tape to attach the soda straw to the edge of one side of the plastic bag.

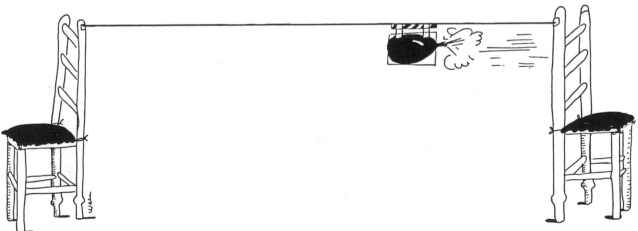

(Activity continued on page 68.)

Activity

Use duct tape to attach one end of a 15-foot length of fishing line to the back of a chair. Run the line through the straw on the edge of the bag and attach the other end of the line to the back of a second chair. Position the chairs so that the line is taut. Slide the bag to the end of the line. Blow up a balloon, pinch the end, and place it in the bag. Release the balloon and watch the balloon rocket fly! Experiment with various balloons, weight of passengers (metal washers in the bags, for example), slope of the line, and a host of other variables.

Science Concepts and Principles

Balloon rockets operate according to Newton's third law of motion. Pressurized air escaping through the mouth (nozzle) of the balloon results in a thrust in the opposite direction. The greater the thrust and the longer the period of time over which it acts, the farther and faster the balloon rocket will fly. This activity is good for investigating the concept of variables and exercising the students' powers of creativity.

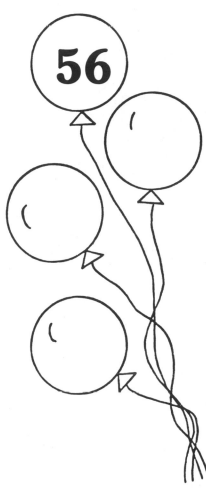

Multistage Balloon Rockets

Materials

Balloons, long style (3)

Quart-size plastic bag

Roll of 10 lb. test monofilament fishing line

Soda straws (12)

Cellophane tape

Duct tape

Paper cups, 8-ounce (2)

Scissors

Preparation

Use cellophane tape to attach the soda straw to the open edge of one side of the plastic bag. Cut off the top 1 inch from both paper cups to make two rings. Use tape to attach a short segment of soda straw to each ring. Make sure the straw segment stands about 1 inch away from the paper ring.

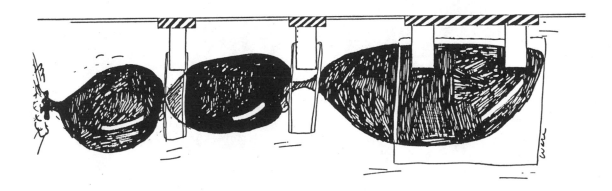

(Activity continued on page 70.)

Activity

Use duct tape to attach one end of a 40-foot length of fishing line to the back of a chair. Run the line through the straws attached to the edge of the bag and paper rings. Attach the other end of the line to the back of a second chair. Position the chairs to make the line taut and slide the bag and rings to the end of the line.

Blow up a balloon, pinch the end, and place it in the bag. Twist the neck of the balloon a few times and then pass it through the first ring. Inflate the second balloon with its butt end (opposite the neck end) inside the same ring. As balloon 2 inflates it will trap the neck of balloon 1 inside the ring and effectively seal it off.

Repeat this procedure for balloon 3 and then launch the whole system. Good luck. This setup may take some fine tuning to get it just right, but when it flies right, the sense of wonder in the crowd, and the sense of satisfaction in the launchers, is worth the effort. Anyway, nobody said science was easy!

Science Concepts and Principles

Balloon rockets operate according to Newton's third law of motion. Pressurized air escaping through the mouth of the balloon results in a thrust in the opposite direction. The extra stages in this activity provide additional excitement, but do not demonstrate any additional concepts with the possible exception of perseverance.

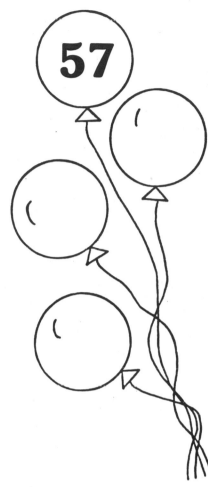

Rocket Boat

Materials

Balloon, long style

Rubber bands (3)

Duct tape

Paper milk carton, ½-gallon

Bathtub or large container of water

Preparation

Stick a 3-inch piece of soda straw into the neck of the balloon and attach the balloon to the straw securely with a rubber band and duct tape.

(Activity continued on page 72.)

Cut the milk carton in half (top to bottom); it is already in the shape of a boat. The top of the carton is the bow of the boat. Punch a small hole in the stern of your boat right down at the floor level. It should be just big enough for the straw to slip through. Push the straw attached to the balloon through the hole from the inside. Put two rubber bands around the boat to keep the balloon inside when it is inflated.

Activity

Inflate the balloon by blowing into the straw sticking through the back of the boat. Put the boat in water and release. Devise a rudder to control the course your boat takes.

Science Concepts and Principles

Newton's third law of motion: For every action there is an opposite and equal reaction. The balloon releases air (action) in one direction, and the boat is propelled (reaction) in the opposite direction.

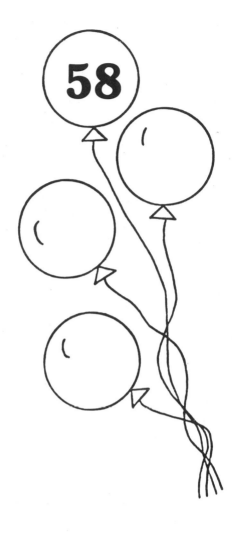

Air Power Soccer

Materials

Balloons, 9-inch (2)

Soda straws (2)

Rubber bands (2)

Duct tape

Ping-pong ball

Preparation

Stick a soda straw into the neck of the balloon and attach the balloon to the straw securely with a rubber band and duct tape. Find a suitable tabletop or floor area for a spirited air soccer game. Edge rails and goals make the game more fun, but rules can be improvised as the game develops. Competitors will inflate their balloons through the straws, point straws toward the ball, and control the airflow by pinching the balloons' necks.

Activity

Two people stand on opposite sides of the gaming area, inflated balloon-straws at the ready. Place the ping-pong ball on the center spot and let the puffs of air begin. May the windiest competitor win.

Science Concepts and Principles

The air escaping through the straw exerts a force strong enough to move the ping-pong ball. According to Newton's second law of motion, when a force (the moving air) is acting on an object (the ping-pong ball) it will move with acceleration. The moving air pushes on the ball and starts it moving. The fact that the moving air can push the ball provides evidence that air has mass, a difficult idea for youngsters to understand.

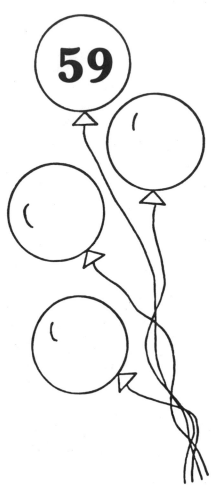

Frictionless Air Scooter

Materials

Retired LP record, 33 1/3-RPM

Empty thread spool (wood if you can find it)

Balloon, 11-inch or larger

Silicone glue

Preparation

Use silicone glue to attach the spool to the center of the LP record. Be careful to line up the holes, and don't let glue fill the hole. Let the scooter dry overnight.

Activity

Slip the mouth of the balloon over the end of the spool. Blow the balloon up by blowing through the hole on the bottom of the scooter. Pinch the balloon shut so that the air doesn't escape while you are getting the frictionless air scooter ready for launch. Place the scooter on the flattest, smoothest surface you can find, perhaps a Formica counter or polished floor. Release the scooter and watch it glide easily along the countertop when given the slightest nudge.

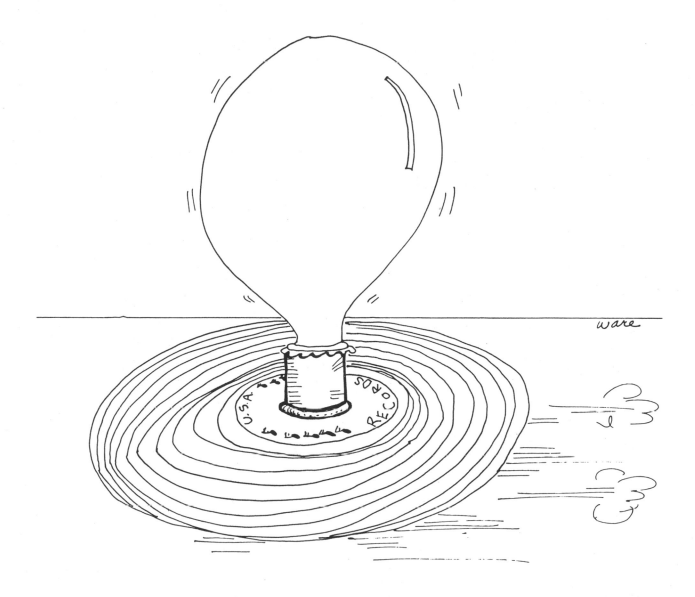

Science Concepts and Principles

Escaping air creates a low friction cushion of air between the surfaces, making it much easier to push your scooter along. Try it without the balloon providing the cushion of air and you will be able to notice a considerable difference. This principle is used in hovercraft, the boats that glide on top of the water as well as land. Air pumped between the hull of the boat and the water provides a cushion, which results in less friction between the hull and water allowing for increased speed and efficiency.

The Balloon Squid

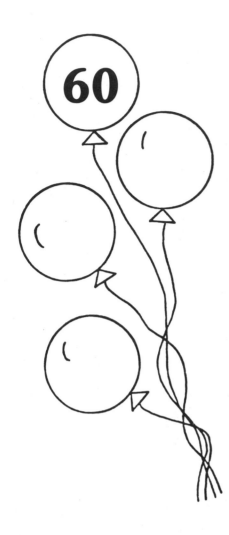

Materials

Balloon, long style

Bathtub or large tub filled with water

Preparation

No advanced preparation is necessary.

Activity

Fill a balloon with water. Hold the balloon under water and release it. The balloon will "jet" off under the water, modeling the propulsion strategy used by squids when they are moving fast. Describe the path of the balloon. Modify the jet outlet with straws or other materials to change the way the "squid" moves.

Science Concepts and Principles

The water in the balloon is under pressure. The pressure inside the balloon is greater than the pressure in the water. Newton's third law of motion is demonstrated: for every action (water in balloon rushing out) there is an opposite (balloon moving) and equal reaction. This activity serves as a model for the way a squid moves in the ocean. Water is discharged under pressure to give this interesting animal rapid movement.

Sound

CONCEPT OF SOUND

The old argument goes, "If a tree falls in a forest, will it make a sound if no one is there to hear?" The argument is more philosophical than scientific. Sound is usually defined as a vibration of matter. If something vibrates, a sound is produced. If you twang a stretched rubber band you hear a sound. If you stretch the rubber band and twang it again you hear a different sound. Why a sound from the rubber band? If you pluck the rubber band you set it in motion. Why the difference in sound between the not-so-tightly stretched rubber band and the tightly stretched rubber band? Stretching the rubber band causes it to vibrate more rapidly. The **frequency** of vibration we know as **pitch**. We speak of low and high pitch. A note toward the left end of a piano keyboard has a lower pitch than a note near the right end. Normally, a note sung by a bass singer is lower pitched than a note sung by a soprano.

A property of sound waves is **amplitude**, which we can think of as how loud sound is. The amount of energy a sound wave carries determines its amplitude or how loud it will be. We can whisper to a friend in the library and hear a soft sound. We can yell to a friend across the street and hear a loud sound. More energy goes into a yell than into a whisper.

The activities in this chapter of the book are designed around the concept of sound. Enjoy.

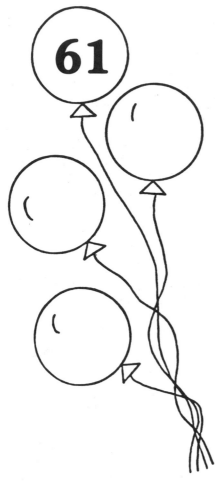

B'loon Toons

Materials

Balloon, 9-inch

Preparation

No advanced preparation is necessary. This activity is a lot of fun, although it may border on being socially unacceptable. If you are musically gifted you can become a balloon virtuoso and play a tune on your balloon. If you can find other talented people you can form a balloon chorus or a balloon marching band and call your group the "Balloonatics."

Activity

Inflate the balloon and pinch its mouth shut with your fingers. Grab the two sides of the neck of the balloon and stretch them out as you slowly release the air. Vary the amount you stretch the neck of the balloon and notice the different sound effects.

Science Concepts and Principles

Sound emanates from vibrating objects. Air rushing past the tightly stretched rubber membrane of the balloon neck starts the rubber vibrating. The vibrating membrane starts the air vibrating, and that vibrating air is what visits our ears to tell us that there is some horrific racket going on. The amount of vibration changes as you vary the amount you stretch the balloon. Stretching the neck of the balloon until the rubber membrane is very tight causes the membrane to vibrate very rapidly. Consequently, the resulting squeal is high pitched because the faster something vibrates, the higher the pitch of the sound it produces. Relaxing the tension on the neck of the balloon produces a raunchy, lower pitched sound emitted from the larger opening. With a little practice (and patience and understanding from your neighbors) you can learn to play scales or popular tunes.

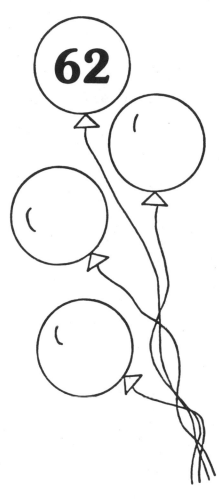

Seeing Sound

Materials

Soup can with both ends removed
Circle cut from a 9-inch balloon
Rubber band
Small piece of broken mirror, 1 inch or less across
Glue (silicone works well)
Flashlight

Preparation

Cut a circle from a balloon large enough to cover one of the open ends of the can. Stretch it moderately tightly and secure it in place with a rubber band. Glue the piece of mirror in the center of the rubber membrane.

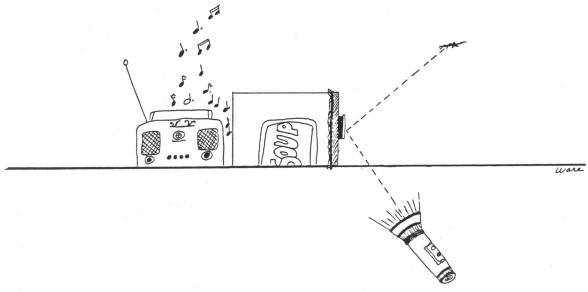

(Activity continued on page 80.)

Activity

Darken the room. Position the can and the flashlight so that the mirror reflects the light onto the wall. Talk, sing, or play a radio into the open end of the can and watch the vibrating light reflection on the wall. A little practice can make this an exciting and interesting demonstration. Keep working on it until the effect is dramatic. You will notice that some pitches really seem to affect the vibration.

Science Concepts and Principles

Sound is vibration. Sound entering the open end of the can causes the air in the can, the balloon membrane, and the attached mirror to vibrate. The vibrating mirror causes the reflected beam of light from the flashlight to jiggle and dance, making sound "visible." It takes a little practice to know just what sounds make the most dramatic "show." Also, a bright flashlight in a dark room is most effective.

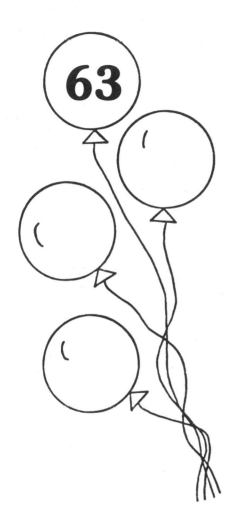

The Phonograph Memory

63

Materials

Balloon, 9-inch, round
Plastic soda straw, cut on diagonal
Masking tape
Phonograph
Phonograph record that isn't too precious

Preparation

Cut the soda straw on a long diagonal so that it is very sharp.

Activity

Inflate the balloon and tie off the end. Use masking tape to attach the soda straw firmly to the side of the balloon. Place the record on the turntable, start the turntable revolving, and slowly and carefully place the sharpened end of the straw into the groove on the record. Listen carefully.

Science Concepts and Principles

The grooves on a record disk are not smooth. You can verify this fact by inspecting a record with a magnifying glass. It's these irregularities that account for the sounds that come off of the record. After all, that's why we bought the thing in the first place. Let's see if we can figure out how it works.

The original recording was "cut" from a perfectly smooth disk of wax. Imagine Louis Armstrong blowing his horn into a device that transforms the vibrations of his music into a series of vibrations of a cutting stylus that is tracing a line in the rotating disk of unmarked wax. All of the bumps and jogs in the groove traced by the stylus are translations of the music.

Once the original is completed, copies are manufactured in plastic for wide distribution. The audiophile brings the record home and reverses the process. She sets the bumpy groove rotating and places a stylus in the groove. The stylus wobbles and bounces in the groove in response to the modulations of the music. Those movements of the stylus are reconverted into pulses of electricity that eventually set a speaker cone to vibrating. The vibrations are interpreted by our hearing mechanism as the dulcet tones of the famous jazz musician.

You are able to pick up the vibrations with your soda-straw needle and amplify them enough to hear just using a balloon resonator on the end of your stylus. After all, that's just the way Edison's Victrola did it over a century ago, and it still works today.

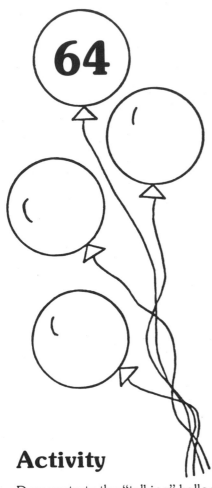

The Talking Balloon

Materials

"Talking" balloon
Coarse twine string, 3-ft.
Magnifier

Preparation

This activity requires some "store bought" supplies. You need to find a store that sells "talking" balloons. Try a good gift card shop or a balloon specialty shop. The "talking" balloon consists of a balloon and a plastic sound strip. You can get "talking" balloons that say, "I Love You," "Have a Nice Day," "Happy Birthday," and so forth. Read the directions carefully and practice a few times so you can get the results you want whenever you want them.

Activity

Demonstrate the "talking" balloon by running your clenched index finger and thumbnails the length of the sound strip attached to the balloon. Have people guess what makes the sound they hear. After a little inquiry you might have people inspect the strip with a magnifying glass. They will be able to report that the plastic strip has "ridges" and that these ridges must somehow be responsible for the sound. Have a very keen observer attempt to describe the pattern of the ridges. When people are convinced that the pattern of the ridges makes a difference, have them predict what will happen when you replace the sound strip with a piece of course twine string. Try it and hear what happens.

Science Concepts and Principles

The balloon in this activity is simply a sound amplifier. The sound strip makes sound in much the same way the grooves in a phonograph record are responsible for the sound. In a record, the grooves are uneven in their depth and width and were made that way by a recording stylus in the studio control room. The needle tracing the grooves vibrates in the same pattern as the original sound vibrations in the studio, making the recording stylus move. An amplifier makes the sound louder and a speaker system, depending on the quality, replicates the original sound. The sound strip is a short recording. The vibrations have caused a stylus to cut grooves in the plastic that replicate the pattern of the original sound. The sound you hear is a purely mechanical reproduction. Your thumbnail and fingernail pulling over the length of the sound strip set up a vibration. That sound is very small, but is amplified somewhat by the balloon. The twine will make a sound also, but because the pattern of the twine is fairly regular the sound will not be nearly so impressive as the sound of the "talking" balloon.

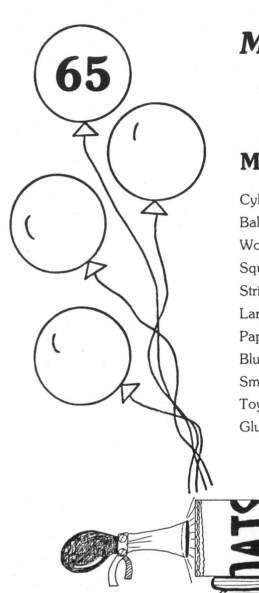

Model of the Ear

65

Materials

Cylindrical box (such as an oatmeal box)

Balloon, 9-inch

Wooden dowel rod, 6 inches long (anvil), 1/8-inch

Square of balsa wood, ½-by-¼-by-½ inches (hammer)

Strip of balsa wood, ¼-by-¼-by-½ inches (stirrup)

Large rubber band

Paper drinking cup

Blue food coloring

Small lump of clay

Toy horn

Glue, silicone is good

(Activity continued on page 84.)

Preparation

Cut off both ends from the oatmeal box. Cut a circle out of the balloon and stretch the circle over one end of the box, securing it with a rubber band. Glue the square of balsa to the middle of the balloon membrane. Cut the dowel rod to a length of about 6 inches and glue one end of the rod to the balsa square on the balloon. Glue the strip of balsa wood to the end of the rod not attached to the balloon membrane. Position the assembly on top of some books stacked to just the right height so that the end of the dowel rod will point down and hang about an inch above the tabletop. You may need to put pinches of clay against the sides of the oatmeal box so that it doesn't roll about. Next, position the cup on the tabletop so that it just comes in contact with the dowel rod assembly. Fill the cup with water and add some food coloring. When the model is correctly adjusted, blowing the horn into the open end of the oatmeal carton causes the balloon membrane to vibrate, which causes the dowel rod assembly to vibrate and hit against the side of the cup. Then water in the cup vibrates so that you can see the vibration as ripples on the surface of the water.

Science Concepts and Principles

The model of the ear is illustrated. The horn represents some sound entering the aural canal (oatmeal box) and setting the eardrum (balloon membrane) into motion. The balsa square represents the hammer, the dowel rod the anvil, and the balsa strip the stirrup, the three small bones of the inner ear. The cup with water represents the inner ear cochlea and fluid that is set into motion when sounds enter the ear. In our ears, these pulses of the fluid in the inner ear are sensed by nerve endings, and electrical nerve impulses carry the message to our brain, giving us the sensation of hearing.

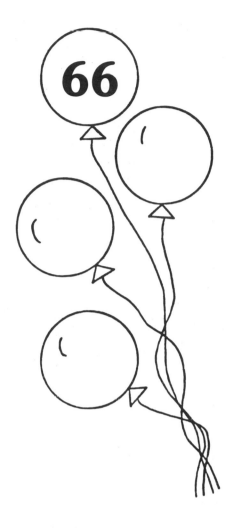

Squeaky Voice

Materials

Helium balloon

Preparation

This activity takes no preparation except to keep your eyes open for a helium balloon. A balloon store or novelty store is a good place to start looking. Ball parks, fairs, and other festive events usually spawn helium balloons as well. Or you can buy a small tank of helium from a party supply store and make a few helium balloons yourself.

NOTE: Helium is a safe gas. It is inert, which means it will not combine with anything else to produce a chemical reaction. It will not burn or explode. It is not toxic to people. It can be inhaled safely as long as it is not the only gas breathed. As we're sure you know, a steady supply of oxygen is required by all of us to maintain consciousness, so, when you inhale helium from a balloon, be sure to take several breaths of air between helium breaths.

Activity

You can amuse your children and amaze your pets with this activity. Untie or otherwise open the neck of a helium balloon. Put the open end of the balloon in your mouth and gently release the gas as you inhale. Turn to your audience and recite a nursery rhyme or other short piece. The pitch of your voice will be raised to an always comical falsetto pitch.

Science Concepts and Principles

Speech is accomplished when the vocal cords in the larynx are set to vibrating by the passage of breath through them. The speed of sound is different in the helium gas, therefore, the wavelengths that resonate in the various cavities in the sound path are shortened. The result is the higher pitched voice.

Static Electricity

CONCEPT OF STATIC ELECTRICITY

The idea of static electricity is not new. A Greek philosopher, Thales, observed over two thousand years ago that if he rubbed a piece of amber with a material, such as wool, it attracted small, light objects. This is the apparent beginning of a long series of observations that led to the discovery of electricity. The word, "electricity" comes from the Greek word, "electron," which means, ... guess what? "Amber."

If you comb your hair on a dry day you can experience the phenomenon of static electricity. Particularly if you have just washed and dried your hair and you try to comb or brush it you find that it tries to fly in all directions. What you have done with the comb or brush is to put an electrical charge on your hair. Because all your hairs received the same charge they repel each other. That's one thing we know about static electricity: like charges repel and unlike charges attract.

The activities in this chapter deal with the concept of static electricity. Many people freak out when they hear the word "electricity" because they think they might get shocked. You can, in fact, receive a small shock when you touch something that is electrically charged or if you are electrically charged and the thing you touch is metallic and not charged. Perhaps you have experienced walking across a carpet on a dry day, touching a doorknob, and receiving a small shock. In this case, you have picked up a charge by shuffling along on the carpet. The discharge happened as you touched the metal doorknob. Don't worry about getting shocked in this series of activities. If you receive a little shock you definitely will not be hurt and usually you won't even feel it.

Another word. Activities involving static electricity work best when there is not much humidity in the air. If you live in a fairly humid place you will want to do these activities on the driest of days.

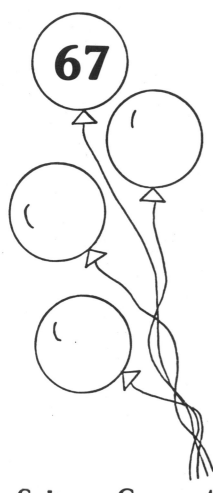

Charging a Balloon

Materials

Balloon

Preparation

No advanced preparation is necessary.

Activity

Inflate the balloon and pinch the end shut. Rub the balloon on your hair or sweater. Hold the balloon close to but not touching your hair. Watch in a mirror as your hair stands on end.

Science Concepts and Principles

Rubber balloons easily pick up extra electrons, giving them a net negative static electric charge. Hair, on the other hand, easily relinquishes electrons, giving it a net positive static electric charge. There is an attractive interaction between the hair and balloon because of the opposite electrical charges. You may notice the same thing when you run a rubber comb through your hair on a dry, cold day, particularly if your hair is not very oily. The comb can make the hairs on your head frizzy and unmanageable.

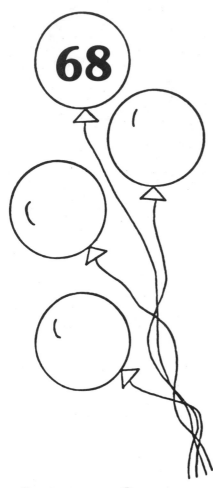

Static Sticky Business

Materials

Balloon

Preparation

No advanced preparation is necessary. Activities involving static electricity work best in conditions of low humidity.

Activity

Inflate a balloon and tie off its end. Rub it against a wool sweater or in your hair. Stick the balloon to a wall or ceiling.

Science Concepts and Principles

No, it's not the oil in your hair that causes the balloon to stick to the wall. Static electricity is produced on the rubber balloon by rubbing it on various materials. The balloon attracts opposite charges in the wall.

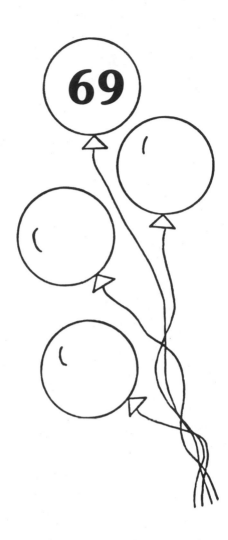

Bending Water

Materials

Balloon

Thin stream of running water

Preparation

No advanced preparation is necessary. This activity works best in conditions of low humidity.

Activity

Inflate a balloon and rub it in your hair. Hold the balloon close to a thin stream of running water. See if the water stream is affected by the presence of the charged balloon.

Science Concepts and Principles

Rubbing the balloon on the hair, deposits an electrical charge on the balloon. This charge attracts the stream of running water.

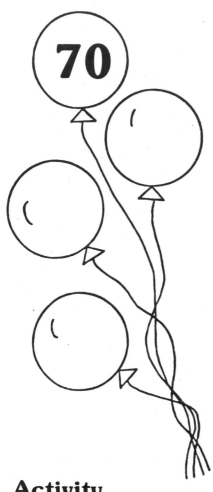

70 Gelatin Stalagmites and Stalactites

Materials

Balloon

Piece of wool

Unflavored gelatin, dry

Glass dish

Preparation

No advanced preparation is necessary. All static electricity activities work best in areas where the humidity is low.

Activity

Pour a small amount of dry, unflavored gelatin into the glass dish. Inflate the balloon and pinch off the end. Rub the balloon with wool. Place the balloon near the gelatin in the dish and watch stalagmites and stalactites form.

Science Concepts and Principles

Rubbing the balloon with the wool deposits an electrical charge on the balloon. The static charge on the balloon attracts the gelatin particles.

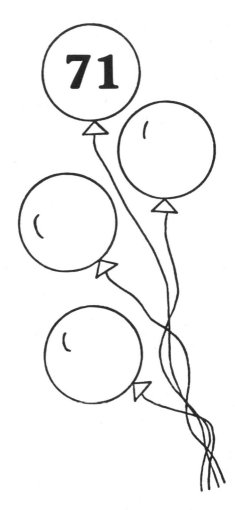

Static Electricity and the No. 2 Pencil

71

Materials

Balloon
Book
Pencil

Preparation

Static electricity is perfectly harmless. Arrange for a day when the humidity is low. Humid conditions affect the action of static electricity, making results less pronounced.

Activity

Open the book a bit and stand it on a table like a tent. Balance the pencil on the book binding. Inflate the balloon, pinch off the end, and rub the balloon vigorously against your hair. Hold the balloon near the pencil and watch the pencil move.

Science Concepts and Principles

Rubbing the balloon on your hair causes a transfer of electrons from your hair to the balloon. Electrons have a negative electrical charge. The buildup of electrical charge is called static electricity.

We experience static electricity sometimes when we walk across a carpeted floor, then receive a slight "shock" when we touch something metallic. This phenomenon is most common in areas where the humidity is low. It's also static electricity that allows us to pick up small bits of paper with a comb that has just been passed through out hair.

Why does the pencil move? The pencil may have an electric charge also. If the charge is the same as the balloon, the pencil will move away. It repels. If the pencil has no charge, the act of bringing the charged balloon near the pencil can cause the charges in the molecules to shift so that the sides of the molecules closest to the balloon will have an induced charge opposite to that of the balloon. The balloon once again attracts the polarized pencil.

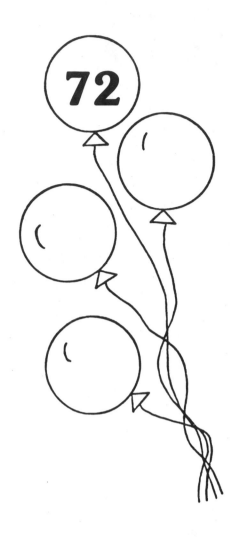

Static Trio

Materials

Balloons (3)

Strings, each 2 feet long (3)

Woolen cloth

Preparation

No advanced preparation is necessary. Activities involving static electricity work best when the humidity is low.

Activity

Inflate the balloons and tie off ends. Tie a string to each balloon. Charge the balloons by rubbing each vigorously with the wool cloth. Hang the three balloons at a common point of the same level and observe their interaction.

Science Concepts and Principles

The balloons all acquire a negative electrical charge as a result of being rubbed with the wool. They all push away from one another because like charges repel. The balloons will stand out from each other and, if conditions are right, not touch. This activity can be very useful if you ever need something that looks like a pawn shop sign.

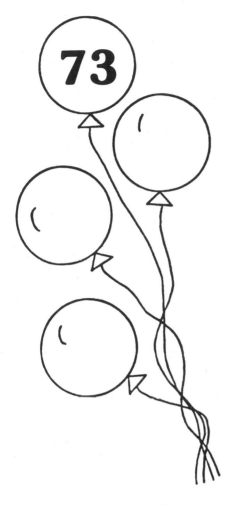

Aluminum Can Races

Materials

Balloon for each participant

Empty aluminum pop can for each participant

Preparation

No advanced preparation is necessary. Static electricity demonstrations, experiments, and applications work best when the humidity is low.

Activity

Each participant should place his or her racer (aluminum can) at the starting line on a level, hard surface, such as a tabletop. Next, the balloons should be inflated and tied off. Contestants should rub their balloons briskly against a wool sweater, skirt, or hair. On the "go" signal contestants should try to pull their racers toward them with the attraction between the balloon and aluminum can. Balloons must remain in front of the can as it is pulled along.

Science Concepts and Principles

The rubbing of the balloon places an electric charge on the surface of the balloon. The charge attracts the lightweight, easily moved, uncharged aluminum can by an induced charge.

Models and Miscellany

Some of the activities in this book do not fit neatly into categories. This section presents a variety of things to do with balloons covering many different concepts. Some are simulations that you can enjoy doing. Some are puzzlers that you can spend some time on and try to figure out an answer. Many of the activities will form the basis for inquiry. If inquiring minds want to know, maybe they can use balloons to help them find out.

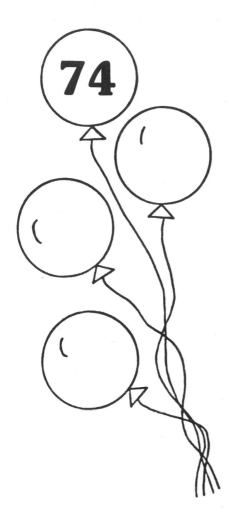

Anatomy of a Sneeze

74

Materials

Balloon, 9-inch

Confetti (100 or so paper punch outs)

Paper to make a funnel

Pin

Preparation

Use a paper punch to punch a bunch of holes in some paper. Any paper will do although colored paper will add interest to the demonstration. Because this demonstration is going to make some mess, it may be a good idea to use paper of a color that will be easily visible against the floor, carpet, or whatever surface you're working on. On the other hand, you may want to select a color that blends in with the surroundings, which will greatly shorten the cleanup time. Draw concentric circles in chalk on the floor so that circles are 5, 10, 20, and 30 inches from the center.

Activity

Make a small funnel out of a piece of paper and use it to put the confetti bits into an uninflated balloon. You may need someone to assist you in this operation. Sometimes balloons can be very uncooperative with their small, long necks. After the confetti is in the balloon, inflate it fully, trying hard to keep as much moisture as possible out of the balloon. (A little tire pump can come in handy for this inflation.) Pinch off the mouth of the balloon. Indicate that you are going to simulate a sneeze. The confetti inside the balloon represents bacteria. Say "Ah—Choo" as you pop the balloon with a pin. Observe where the confetti lands. Students can measure the distance that "bacteria" travels from "ground zero" and prepare a histogram that shows the distribution.

(Activity continued on page 96.)

0-5	6-10	11-15	16-20	21-25	26-30	31-35	36+
			X	X			
		X	X	X			
	X	X	X	X	X		
	X	X	X	X	X		
	X	X	X	X	X	X	
	X	X	X	X	X	X	X
X	X	X	X	X	X	X	X

Distance in inches   0-5   6-10   11-15   16-20   21-25   26-30   31-35   36 +

Science Concepts and Principles

When the balloon bursts, air molecules move outward in all directions as the pressure equalizes almost instantly. Air molecules impact the bits of confetti, sending them flying off in all directions. This serves as an analogy of a sneeze in which the released pressure built up before a sneeze sends particles flying into the air. The use of a tissue to catch the sneeze serves to localize the distribution of particles we expel and helps cut down on the spread of bacteria.

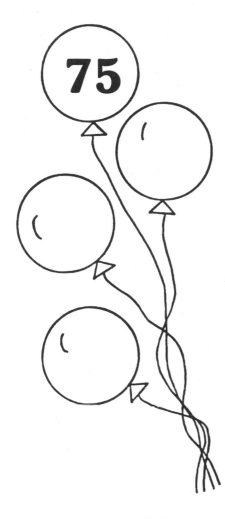

What in the...?

75

Materials

Several balloons, 9-inch

Alligator clip

One-inch pieces of small-diameter plastic or rubber tubing (2)

Plastic soda bottle, 2-liter

Funnel

Sewing needle

Materials to put into balloons, e.g., vermiculite, Rice Krispies, diatomaceous earth

Preparation

Prepare a rubber-guarded alligator clip by slipping a short length of rubber or plastic tubing over each half of the clip jaws. This gadget can be clipped onto the neck of an inflated balloon to hold in the air without damaging the balloon.

This activity promotes lateral thinking. At first students may think the problem is to figure out what's in the balloon, but it's really about figuring out how you got the Rice Krispies into the balloon in the first place.

Here's what you do before class. Use the funnel to put about three cups of vermiculite, Rice Krispies, or diatomaceous earth into the plastic pop bottle. Now blow up a balloon to about 5 inches in diameter. Put the clip on the balloon neck well back from the mouth. Stretch the mouth of the balloon over the mouth of the pop bottle, making sure that it is on there securely. Remove the clip. Invert the bottle-balloon system and gently squeeze the material into the inflated balloon, using little pumping actions to squeeze the sides of the bottle. When it is all in there, squeeze the neck shut and yank the balloon off of the bottle. Carefully let out the extra air so that the balloon is filled with only the material. Tie the balloon off. If the material in the balloon is not a fluid, poke a couple of tiny holes through the neck of the balloon right by the knot. Let your imagination guide your choice of materials to put into balloons. Rice is great. Baking soda is very provocative.

Activity

Bring several funny balloons to class and let the students examine them to determine what is inside. Then let them try to figure out how to make a balloon of that type. BUT, don't tell how you did it!

Science Concept or Principle

This activity doesn't really demonstrate a principle or develop an important concept, but it can really stimulate creativity and analytical thinking. Let the students try their ideas for filling balloons with interesting materials. The joy of this activity is struggling with the engineering problem of getting strange materials into a balloon.

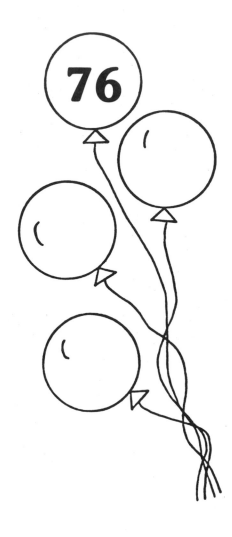

76

Egg Drop Balloon Experiment

Materials

Balloons, ten per participant or team

Milk carton

Egg, one per participant or team

Rubber bands

Masking tape

String

Preparation

This is a good inquiry activity. There are probably many structures that can be constructed to protect a raw egg from breaking. No advance preparation is necessary other than to find a location from which eggs can be dropped and a batch of callous bystanders who can watch and laugh at being splattered by raw eggs if things go wrong. Some clean up may be required.

Activity

Using the materials, construct a structure that will contain and protect a raw egg dropped from a height of 10 feet. Suggest using partially inflated balloons as cushioning material in the milk carton. What arrangement affords the greatest protection?

Science Concepts and Principles

Inertia is the culprit that causes fragile things to break as they come to a very fast stop. A falling body (the egg and its container) gains momentum and that momentum translates to force as the object hits an immovable object (the ground). The shell of an egg is fragile enough that you can predict with some certainty it will break if dropped onto the earth from a height of 10 feet. The force of impact is greater than the shell can withstand. It's been said many times that it isn't the fall that breaks the egg, but the sudden stop. The force of impact equals the mass of the egg multiplied times the acceleration ($F = ma$). To save the egg we can slow the acceleration. By putting a balloon (or several) between the egg and the earth, the time required to bring the egg's velocity to zero will be extended; the acceleration will be reduced. The lower the acceleration, the lower the force. Had Humpty Dumpty only known....

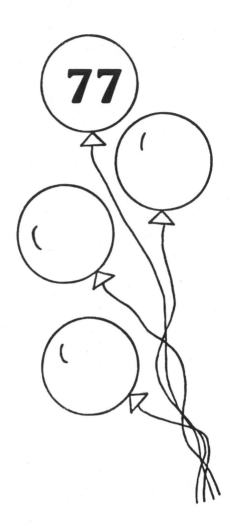

Water Lift

Materials

Balloon, 7-inch (or plastic bag)

Plastic tubing, ¼-inch diameter, 2 or 3 feet long

Funnel, 3-inch plastic

Book (or other modest weight)

Plastic tumbler, 8-ounce

Dish basin

Water

Rubber bands

Duct tape

Preparation

This is a pretty complicated setup and is likely to leak all over everything if you aren't careful. Make sure that all your seals are tight. Just in case, have paper toweling or sponges ready to mop up spills. Don't use a precious book because it might get wet. You can find plastic tubing among the aquarium supplies in a pet store.

Attach the balloon or plastic bag to one end of the tubing. Use rubber bands and duct tape to get it on there securely. Attach the funnel to the other end of the tube; tape it on securely.

Activity

Put the balloon end of the apparatus in the basin and place a weight on top of the balloon. Keep the funnel end of the apparatus elevated above the object as you pour water into it. Water will enter and expand the balloon. Continue to pour water into the system to see if you can lift the book. Try pressing on the balloon to push the water back up the tube. Notice how much pressure you have to exert.

(Activity continued on page 100.)

Science Concepts and Principles

This activity illustrates the principle of hydraulics. The pressure of the water in the balloon depends on the height of water in the tube. The height of the column is called the pressure head.

Increased pressure acts evenly throughout a closed system in which a liquid is placed. If you exert a force on a small area (like the tube in your system), that force is transmitted throughout the system. Even a low pressure is enough to lift a substantial weight because the pressure is acting over a relatively large area.

For example, in the apparatus described above, let's imagine a column of water in the tubing weighs one pound and the tubing has a cross section of 1 square inch. The 1 pound of water increases the pressure throughout the system by 1 pound by square inch. When the pressure acts on an area of 10 square inches, it produces a force of 10 pounds (one pound per square inch). This simple hydraulic system has multiplied your force of 1 pound by a factor of 10.

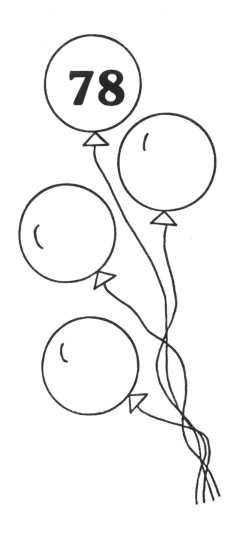

Expanding by Cooling

Materials

Balloon, 9-inch

Measuring tape

Water

Freezer

Preparation

Inflate a balloon with water.

Activity

Measure the circumference of a water balloon. Place it in a freezer for six hours or longer. Remove the balloon from the freezer and measure the circumference.

Science Concepts and Principles

Water is a pretty amazing substance with a strange physical property. As water is cooled, it contracts, like we would expect. But before freezing at about 32°F (0°C), it begins to expand! And then when it changes state from liquid to solid, it expands even more—about 10 percent. The frozen water balloon will actually be larger than the liquid water balloon.

This phenomenon can cause problems. If water pipes aren't protected from winter cold, they can freeze and burst. Also, the water used to cool automobile engines has antifreeze added in most locales to prevent the water from freezing and bursting our radiator pipes and engine blocks during severe winter conditions.

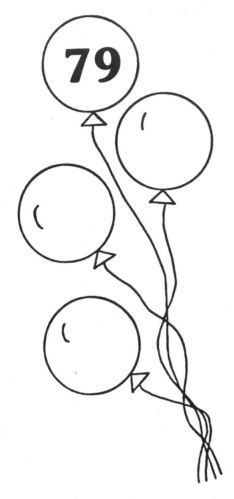

The Dry Ice Magical Inflation

Materials

Balloon
Dry ice (be careful!)

Tools

Hammer
Spoon
Towel

Preparation

Dry ice is available from a variety of sources, including ice cream stores and some supermarkets. Dry ice should be handled with caution because the temperature of dry ice is about -130°F. Use heavy gloves or an implement, such as tongs, with dry ice. Contact with the skin for even a short period of time can cause severe burns (frostbite). You will need to break up the dry ice so that it will fit easily into a balloon neck. This can be done by wrapping the chunk of dry ice in a towel and pounding it with a hammer until pieces small enough to put into the balloon are produced.

Activity

Use a spoon to place several small pieces of dry ice in an uninflated balloon. **Caution:** Do not handle dry ice with your bare hands. Severe burns can result. Tie off the balloon and watch it inflate.

Science Concepts and Principles

Dry ice is carbon dioxide in a solid form. At standard atmospheric pressure carbon dioxide exists in two phases, solid or gas. Materials that go directly from a solid to gaseous state are said to sublime. The gaseous state of carbon dioxide takes up many times more space than carbon dioxide in the solid state. The balloon expands to accommodate the expanding gaseous state of the carbon dioxide.

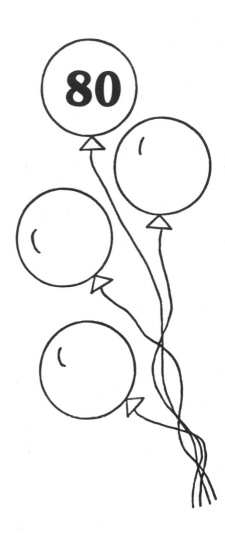

Lung Model

Materials

Clear plastic quart tumbler

Walnut-sized lump of modeling clay

"Y" tube from aquarium shop or science supply store

Balloons, 7-inch (2)

Balloon, 11-inch

Large rubber band

Small rubber bands (2)

Preparation

This activity has a difficult preparation because you must find a suitable plastic container that is clear and rigid; 2-liter pop bottles are not rigid enough. This is the point in the preparation when it is

(Activity continued on page 104.)

great to know somebody with a shop who can drill a hole in the bottom of the tumbler. Be careful if you undertake this task yourself.

Bore or drill a hole into the bottom of the tumbler. It should be a little larger than the diameter of your "Y" tube. Attach a small balloon to each leg of the "Y," using the small rubber bands. Put the tube inside the tumbler and insert the bottom branch of the "Y" through the hole. Seal off leaks with modeling clay.

Cut the large balloon in half. Pull the bottom half of the balloon over the open mouth of the tumbler and secure it in place with a large rubber band.

Activity

The rubber balloon covering the open bottom of the jar is a model of the diaphragm. To simulate breathing, grab the center of the rubber diaphragm and pull down. Observe the "lungs" inflate each time the diaphragm is pulled down.

Science Concepts and Principles

When we breathe, a powerful muscle below our rib cage, called the diaphragm, contracts. The contraction of the diaphragm actually causes the lung cavity inside the rib cage to increase in volume. Air rushes in to fill the increased volume. We call that rush of air a breath. When the diaphragm relaxes, it once again arches up into the bottom of the rib cage, putting pressure on the air in the lungs. The unused air and by-products of respiration are pushed out through our mouths and noses, and the process is ready to repeat.

In this model, the lungs are represented by the two balloons attached to the "Y" tube. The balloon stretched over the bottom of the bottle is the diaphragm. The bottle is the rib cage and the single branch of the "Y" is the trachea. If you try to blow air into the top of the "Y" tube you will have little success in inflating the lungs. Simply pulling the balloon down from the bottom of the tumbler will make the balloons expand easily.

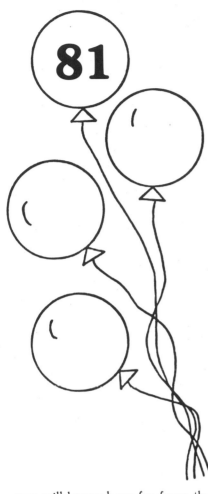

Balloon Optics

Materials

Balloons, 9-inch, light-colored (2)

Felt marker (black is best)

Water

Strip of paper (½ inch by 3 inches)

Preparation

No advanced preparation is necessary.

Activity

Write the words CARBON DIOXIDE on the strip of paper using capital letters. Inflate one balloon with water and the other with air. Look at the words through the balloons. Experiment so that you will know how far from the paper to hold the balloon. Note the differences. Describe what you see.

Science Concepts and Principles

The velocity of light is different in different media. Water slows the speed of light, bending the path of the light in a process known as refraction. The result is that the water balloon acts as a lens, and it reverses the image of the words. Strangely, though, the word "DIOXIDE" looks the same when reversed but "CARBON" does not. The peculiar symmetry of the letters in "DIOXIDE" adds to the interest of this demonstration. The air balloon will not behave as a lens, so the words look the same with or without looking through the balloon.

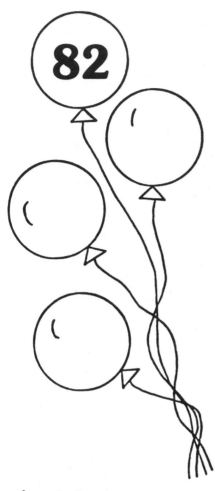

82

Whose Lungs Have Most Hot Air?

Materials

Balloon, 11-inch, one for each participant

Cloth measuring tape (optional)

Preparation

This activity requires very little preparation. You should know ahead of time that an exact measurement of lung volume is not possible using balloons, but comparisons can be made. You need to remember that students long to be "normal." They become concerned if their lung capacities are dramatically different than their peers. Emphasize that there is a large range of "normal."

Activity

Give each student a balloon. Have them stretch and inflate them several times to make them more pliable. Each person inhales as deeply as possible then exhales one breath into the balloon. Measure to see which student had greatest lung volume. It is not necessary to do an actual physical measurement. Simply observing the differences in sizes will be sufficient. However, if you wish to graph results that's o.k. too. Remember, this is not a contest.

Science Concepts and Principles

The volume of air a person can transfer to a balloon in one breath is called vital capacity. Vital capacity is a measure that indicates overall respiratory fitness of people. The lungs will actually hold more than that, but it is not possible to completely empty the lungs with even the most forceful exhalation.

Comparison between students can be meaningful because all participants will have inflated their balloons under essentially the same conditions. An interesting inquiry exercise is to encourage students to speculate on what factors might contribute to large lung volumes. You can collect data and correlate it with sex, height, age, exercise regimens, etc. It turns out that the most reliable predictor of the amount of hot air a person is full of is height.

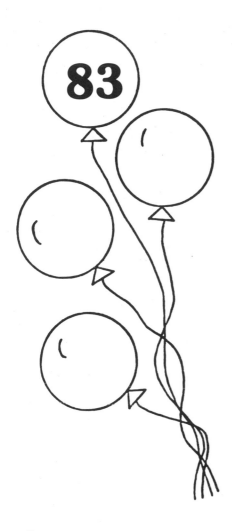

83

Whose Lungs Have Most Hot Air? Part II

Materials

Small plastic trash bags (one for each participant)

Cloth measuring tapes

Preparation

This activity is the same as the previous one except plastic bags replace the balloons. This activity is different from the previous one in that a more exact measurement of vital capacity is possible. Because the plastic bags are not elastic, like the balloons, students are not compressing the air into the "bags" but merely filling them. You need to remember that students long to be "normal." They become concerned if their lung capacities are dramatically less or more than their peers. Emphasize that there is a large range of "normal."

Activity

Give each student a small plastic bag. Have them bunch up the open end of the bag so that a "mouth" is made into which the breath can be exhaled. Each person inhales as deeply as possible then exhales one breath into the bag. Clamp down on the opening to the bag so that no air escapes, run the hand down to trap the air in the bag so that it forms a roughly spherical shape. It is difficult to measure the volumes of air in a meaningful way, though you can try if you wish. It is generally sufficient to compare and rank order volumes visually.

Science Concepts and Principles

The volume of an inflated bag is an indirect measure of vital capacity. Again, this isn't an exact measure of lung volume, however, because it isn't possible for a person to exhale all of the air from his or her lungs. But it can provide a pretty good approximation of vital capacity for information and comparison.

Appendix A: Explanation of Correlation of Activities to Current Elementary Science Textbook Series

The appendixes present correlations between the activities in the book and current elementary science textbook series. Included are the top four series and three other series that have a late copyright date and whose scope and sequence charts were readily available. The correlations given here should not be considered exhaustive but should serve as a guideline for teachers. Only elementary series were correlated. Junior high and high school teachers should find it relatively easy to correlate the content area of each activity to the textbook series or program that they use.

A 1985-86 report by Iris R. Weiss titled, *National Survey of Science and Mathematics Education*, indicated that textbooks play a central role in science instruction. The results from a survey suggested that almost 70 percent of kindergarten through third-grade classes use textbooks and almost 90 percent of fourth- through sixth-grade classes use them. The survey further identified the most-used textbook series. A "market share" report of usage in kindergarten through sixth-grade indicated the following:

Series	Percent of Classes
Silver Burdett & Ginn	26
D. C. Heath	15
Merrill Publishing Company	14
Holt, Rinehart, and Winston	10
McGraw Hill	7
Scott, Foresman	4
Laidlaw	2
Prentice Hall	1

Looking at the results of this survey in another way, the top four textbook series (Silver Burdett & Ginn, D. C. Heath, Merrill Publishing Company, and Holt, Rinehart, and Winston) represent a 65 percent share of the market.

TEXTBOOK SERIES USED IN THE CORRELATION

Addison-Wesley Science, *Level K; Level 1; Level 2; Level 3; Level 4; Level 5; Level 6*, 1989.

Harcourt Brace Jovanovich, Nova Edition, *HBJ Science Level R; HBJ Science Level 1; HBJ Science Level 2; HBJ Science Level 3; HBJ Science Level 4; HBJ Science Level 5; HBJ Science Level 6*, 1988.

Heath, D. C., *Heath Science, Level K; Heath Science, Level 1; Heath Science, Level 2; Heath Science, Level 3; Heath Science, Level 4; Heath Science, Level 5; Heath Science, Level 6,* 1988.

Holt, Rinehart, and Winston, *Holt Science, Level K; Holt Science, Level 1; Holt Science, Level 2; Holt Science, Level 3; Holt Science, Level 4; Holt Science, Level 5; Holt Science, Level 6,* 1989.

Macmillan Publishing Company, *Journeys in Science, Level K; Journeys in Science, Level 1; Journeys in Science, Level 2; Journeys in Science, Level 3; Journeys in Science, Level 4; Journeys in Science, Level 5; Journeys in Science, Level 6,* 1988.

Merrill Publishing Company, *Merrill Science, Level K; Merrill Science, Level 1; Merrill Science, Level 2; Merrill Science, Level 3; Merrill Science, Level 4; Merrill Science, Level 5; Merrill Science, Level 6,* 1989.

Silver Burdett & Ginn, *Silver Burdett & Ginn Science Level K; Silver Burdett & Ginn Science Level 1; Silver Burdett & Ginn Science Level 2; Silver Burdett & Ginn Science Level 3; Silver Burdett & Ginn Science Level 4; Silver Burdett & Ginn Science Level 5; Silver Burdett & Ginn Science Level 6,* 1988.

Appendix B: Correlation of Activities with Addison-Wesley K-6 Series

Activity	Concept	Grade Level/Chapter
1. Shhh! The Balloons Have Ears	air pressure	2
2. The Stubborn Balloon	air pressure	2
3. The Inside-Out Balloon	air pressure	2
4. A Balloon Trick	air pressure	2
5. Balloon in a Bottle	air pressure	2
6. Betcha Can't!	air pressure	2
7. Warming Up	heat	4
8. The Incredible Non-shrinking Balloon	heat	4
9. The Incredible Shrinking Balloon	heat	4
10. The Credible Shrinking Balloon	heat	4
11. The Old Balloon-in-the-Bottle Trick	air pressure	2
12. The Old Balloon-out-of-the-Bottle Trick	air pressure	2
13. Hot and Cold	heat	4
14. The Soup Can Trick	air pressure	2
15. Canned Hot Air	air pressure	2
16. The Puffing Jug	air pressure	2
17. The Uplifting Experience	air pressure	2
18. The Second Uplifting Experience	air pressure	2
19. Balloon Cushion	air pressure	2
20. Balloon Megalift	air pressure	2
21. Son of Balloon Megalift	air pressure	2
22. Son of Balloon Megalift: A Success Story	air pressure	2
23. The Old Self-Inflating Balloon Stunt	chemical reaction	3

Activity	Concept	Grade Level/Chapter
24. The Other Self-Inflating Balloon Trick	chemical reaction	3
25. Reversible Balloon	chemical reaction	3
26. Mmmm, Mmmm, Good!	chemical reaction	3
27. The Air We Breathe	chemical reaction	3
28. Float or Sink Balloon	density	4
29. The Cartesian Diver	density	4
30. Hot Air Balloon	density	4
31. Floating Balloon	density	4
32. ... Like a Lead Balloon	gravity	5
33. Gravity Balloons	gravity	5
34. Bouncing Balloons	physical change/properties	3
35. What Goes Up Must Come Down	gravity	5
36. Balloon Races	gravity	5
37. Comparing Gases	gravity	5
38. Blowing in the Wind	gravity	5
39. A Growing Line	physical change/properties	3
40. How Did the Letters Grow?	physical change/properties	3
41. Our Expanding Universe	universe	K
42. Air Has Mass	gravity	5
43. Two Balloons In One	physical change/properties	3
44. The Discrepant Event	air pressure	2
45. A Piercing Moment	physical properties	3
46. A Piercing Moment: Act II	physical properties	3
47. Are Balloons Airtight?	phys. change/properties/permeability	3

Activity	Concept	Grade Level/Chapter
48. Semipermeable Membranes	phys. change/properties/permeability	3
49. The Spouting Water Balloon	water pressure	2
50. Water Balloon Toss	-	-
51. Jet Propulsion	propulsion	5
52. Zoom Balloons	propulsion	5
53. Balloons and Marbles	propulsion	5
54. Balloon Time	propulsion	5
55. Balloon Rockets	propulsion	5
56. Multi-Stage Balloon Rockets	propulsion	5
57. Rocket Boat	propulsion	5
58. Air Power Soccer	propulsion	5
59. Frictionless Air Scooter	propulsion	5
60. The Balloon Squid	propulsion	5
61. B'loon Toons	sound	1
62. Seeing Sound	sound	1
63. The Phonograph Memory	sound	1
64. The Talking Balloon	sound	1
65. Model of the Ear	ear model	K
66. Squeaky Voice	sound	1
67. Charging a Balloon	static electricity	4
68. Static Sticky Business	static electricity	4
69. Bending Water	static electricity	4
70. Gelatin Stalagmites and Stalactites	static electricity	4
71. Static Electricity and the No. 2 Pencil	static electricity	4

Activity	Concept	Grade Level/Chapter
72. Static Trio	static electricity	4
73. Aluminum Can Races	static electricity	4
74. Anatomy of a Sneeze	disease	6
75. What in the...?	inquiry	-
76. Egg Drop Balloon Experiment	inquiry	-
77. Water Lift	water pressure	2
78. Expanding by Cooling	phys. change/properties	3
79. Dry Ice Magical Inflation	physical change/properties	3
80. Lung Model	lung/model	K
81. Balloon Optics	refraction	6
82. Whose Lungs Have Most Hot Air?	lung/model	K
83. Whose Lungs Have Most Hot Air? Part II	lung/model	K

Appendix C: Correlation of Activities with Harcourt, Brace, and Jovanovich K-6 Series

Activity	Concept	Grade Level/Chapter
1. Shhh! The Balloons Have Ears	air pressure	
2. The Stubborn Balloon	air pressure	
3. The Inside-Out Balloon	air pressure	
4. A Balloon Trick	air pressure	
5. Balloon in a Bottle	air pressure	
6. Betcha Can't!	air pressure	
7. Warming Up	heat	
8. The Incredible Non-shrinking Balloon	heat	
9. The Incredible Shrinking Balloon	heat	
10. The Credible Shrinking Balloons	air pressure	
11. The Old Balloon-in-the-Bottle Trick	air pressure	
12. The Old Balloon-out-of-the-Bottle Trick	air pressure	
13. Hot and Cold	heat	
14. The Soup Can Trick	air pressure	
15. Canned Hot Air	air pressure/heat	1(unit 10)
16. The Puffing Jug	air pressure	
17. The Uplifting Experience	air pressure	
18. The Second Uplifting Experience	air pressure	
19. Balloon Cushion	air pressure	
20. Balloon Megalift	air pressure	
21. Son of Balloon Megalift	air pressure	
22. Son of Balloon Megalift: A Success Story	air pressure	

Activity	Concept	Grade Level/Chapter
23. The Old Self-Inflating Balloon Stunt	chemical reaction	5(unit 5)
24. The Other Self-Inflating Balloon Trick	chemical reaction	5(unit 5)
25. Reversible Balloon	chemical reaction	5(unit 5)
26. Mmmm, Mmmm, Good!	chemical reaction	5(unit 5)
27. The Air We Breathe	chemical reaction	5(unit 5)
28. Float or Sink Balloons	density	-
29. The Cartesian Diver	density	-
30. Hot Air Balloon	density	-
31. Floating Balloon	density	-
32. ...Like a Lead Balloon	gravity	1(unit 10)
33. Gravity Balloons	gravity	1(unit 10)
34. Bouncing Balloons	physical change/properties	-
35. What Goes Up Must Come Down	gravity	1(unit 10)
36. Balloon Races	gravity	1(unit 10)
37. Comparing Gases	gravity	1(unit 10)
38. Blowing in the Wind	gravity	1(unit 10)
39. A Growing Line	physical change/properties	-
40. How Did the Letters Grow?	physical change/properties	-
41. Our Expanding Universe	universe	2(unit 8), 3(unit 1), 4(unit 8), 5(unit 3)
42. Air Has Mass	gravity	1(unit 10)
43. Two Balloons in One	inquiry	all
44. The Discrepant Event	air pressure	-
45. A Piercing Moment	physical properties	-

Activity	Concept	Grade Level/Chapter
46. A Piercing Moment: Act II	physical properties	-
47. Are Balloons Air Tight?	phys. change/properties/permeability	-
48. Semipermeable Membranes	phys. change/properties/permeability	-
49. The Spouting Water Balloon	water pressure	-
50. Water Balloon Toss	-	-
51. Jet Propulsion	propulsion	1(unit 9), 5(unit 3)
52. Zoom Balloons	propulsion	1(unit 9), 5(unit 3)
53. Balloons and Marbles	propulsion	1(unit 9), 5(unit 3)
54. Balloon Time	propulsion	1(unit 9), 5(unit 3)
55. Balloon Rockets	propulsion	1(unit 9), 5(unit 3)
56. Multi-stage Balloon Rockets	propulsion	1(unit 9), 5(unit 3)
57. Rocket Boat	propulsion	1(unit 9), 5(unit 3)
58. Air Power Soccer	propulsion	1(unit 9), 5(unit 3)
59. Frictionless Air Scooter	propulsion	1(unit 9), 5(unit 3)
60. The Balloon Squid	propulsion	1(unit 9), 5(unit 3)
61. B'loon Toons	sound	2(unit 6), 4(unit 2)
62. Seeing Sound	sound	2(unit 6), 4(unit 2)
63. The Phonograph Memory	sound	2(unit 6), 4(unit 2)
64. The Talking Balloon	sound	2(unit 6), 4(unit 2)
65. Model of the Ear	ear model	K
66. Squeaky Voice	sound	2(unit 6), 4(unit 2)
67. Charging a Balloon	static electricity	6
68. Static Sticky Business	static electricity	6

Activity	Concept	Grade Level/Chapter
69. Bending Water	static electricity	6
70. Gelatin Stalagmites and Stalactites	static electricity	6
71. Static Electricity and the No. 2 Pencil	static electricity	6
72. Static Trio	static electricity	6
73. Aluminum Can Races	static electricity	6
74. Anatomy of a Sneeze	disease	-
75. What in the...?	inquiry	all
76. Egg Drop Balloon Experiment	inquiry	all
77. Water Lift	pressure	-
78. Expanding by Cooling	phys. change/properties	-
79. Dry Ice Magical Inflation	physical change/properties	-
80. Lung Model	lung, model	K, 5
81. Balloon Optics	refraction	4(unit 3)
82. Whose Lungs Have Most Hot Air?	lung, model	K, 5
83. Whose Lungs Have Most Hot Air? Part II	lung, model	K, 5

Appendix D: Correlation of Activities with Heath K-6 Series

Activity	Concept	Grade Level/Chapter
1. Shhh! The Balloons Have Ears	air pressure	1
2. The Stubborn Balloon	air pressure	1
3. The Inside-Out Balloon	air pressure	1
4. A Balloon Trick	air pressure	1
5. Balloon in a Bottle	air pressure	1
6. Betcha Can't!	air pressure	1
7. Warming Up	heat	-
8. The Incredible Non-shrinking Balloon	heat	-
9. The Incredible Shrinking Balloon	heat	-
10. The Credible Shrinking Balloons	heat	1
11. The Old Balloon-in-the-Bottle Trick	air pressure	1
12. The Old Balloon-out-of-the-Bottle Trick	air pressure	1
13. Hot and Cold	heat	-
14. The Soup Can Trick	air pressure	1
15. Canned Hot Air	air pressure	1
16. The Puffing Jug	air pressure	1
17. The Uplifting Experience	air pressure	1
18. The Second Uplifting Experience	air pressure	1
19. Balloon Cushion	air pressure	6(chapter 5)
20. Balloon Megalift	air pressure	1
21. Son of Balloon Megalift	air pressure	1
22. Son of Balloon Megalift: A Success Story	air pressure	1
23. The Old Self-Inflating Balloon Stunt	chemical reaction	6(chapter 5)

119

Activity	Concept	Grade Level/Chapter
70. Gelatin Stalagmites and Stalactites	static electricity	6(chapter6)
71. Static Electricity and the Number 2 Pencil	static electricity	6(chapter 6)
72. Static Trio	static electricity	6(chapter 6)
73. Aluminum Can Races	static electricity	6(chapter 6)
74. Anatomy of a Sneeze	disease	-
75. What in the....?	inquiry	all
76. Egg Drop Balloon Experiment	inquiry	all
77. Water Lift	water pressure	-
78. Expanding by Cooling	phys. change/properties	-
79. Dry Ice Magical Inflation	physical change/properties	-
80. Lung Model	lung/model	5(chapter 11)
81. Balloon Optics	refraction	6(chapters 8-9)
82. Whose Lungs Have Most Hot Air?	lung/model	5(chapter 11)
83. Whose Lungs Have Most Hot Air? Part II	lung/model	5(chapter 11)

Appendix E: Correlation of Activities with Holt K-6 Series

Activity	Concept	Grade Level/Chapter
1. Shhh! The Balloons Have Ears	air pressure	1, 3, 4
2. The Stubborn Balloon	air pressure	1, 3, 4
3. The Inside-Out Balloon	air pressure	1, 3, 4
4. A Balloon Trick	air pressure	1, 3, 4
5. Balloon in a Bottle	air pressure	1, 3, 4
6. Betcha Can't!	air pressure	1, 3, 4
7. Warming Up	heat	-
8. The Incredible Non-shrinking Balloon	heat	-
9. The Incredible Shrinking Balloon	heat	-
10. The Credible Shrinking Balloons	air pressure	1, 3, 4
11. The Old Balloon-in-the-Bottle Trick	air pressure	1, 3, 4
12. The Old Balloon-out-of-the-Bottle Trick	air pressure	1, 3, 4
13. Hot and Cold	heat	-
14. The Soup Can Trick	air pressure	1, 3, 4
15. Canned Hot Air	air pressure	1, 3, 4
16. The Puffing Jug	air pressure	1, 3, 4
17. The Uplifting Experience	air pressure	1, 3, 4
18. The Second Uplifting Experience	air pressure	1, 3, 4
19. Balloon Cushion	air pressure	1, 3, 4
20. Balloon Megalift	air pressure	1, 3, 4
21. Son of Balloon Megalift	air pressure	1, 3, 4
22. Son of Balloon Megalift: A Success Story	air pressure	1, 3, 4
23. The Old Self-Inflating Balloon Stunt	chemical reaction	6(Unit I, chapter 9)
24. The Other Self-Inflating Balloon Trick	chemical reaction	6 (Unit I,chapter 9)

Activity	Concept	Grade Level/Unit
25. Reversible Balloon	chemical reaction	6(unit I, chapter 9)
26. Mmmm, Mmmm, Good!	chemical reaction	6(unit I, chapter 9)
27. The Air We Breathe	chemical reaction	6(unit I, chapter 9)
28. Float or Sink Balloons	density	-
29. The Cartesian Diver	density	-
30. Hot Air Balloon	density	-
31. Floating Balloon	density	-
32. ...Like a Lead Balloon	gravity	-
33. Gravity Balloons	gravity	-
34. Bouncing Balloons	physical change/properties	-
35. What Goes Up Must Come Down	gravity	-
36. Balloon Races	gravity	-
37. Comparing Gases	gravity	-
38. Blowing In The Wind	gravity	-
39. A Growing Line	physical change/properties	-
40. How Did the Letters Grow?	physical change/properties	-
41. Our Expanding Universe	universe	3(unit 1), 5(unit 6)
42. Air Has Mass	gravity	-
43. Two Balloons in One	physical change/properties	-
44. The Discrepant Event	air pressure	1, 3, 4
45. A Piercing Moment	physical properties	-
46. A Piercing Moment: Act II	physical properties	-
47. Are Balloons Air Tight?	phys. change/properties/permeability	-

Activity	Concept	Grade Level/Chapter
48. Semipermeable Membranes	physical change/properties/permeability	-
49. The Spouting Water Balloon	water pressure	1, 3, 4
50. Water Balloon Toss	-	-
51. Jet Propulsion	propulsion	6(unit 1)
52. Zoom Balloons	propulsion	6(unit it 1)
53. Balloons and Marbles	propulsion	6(unit 1)
54. Balloon Time	propulsion	6(unit 1)
55. Balloon Rockets	propulsion	6(unit 1)
56. Multi-stage Balloon Rockets	propulsion	6(unit 1)
57. Rocket Boat	propulsion	6(unit 1)
58. Air Power Soccer	propulsion	6(unit 1)
59. Frictionless Air Scooter	propulsion	6(unit 1)
60. The Balloon Squid	propulsion	6(unit 1)
61. B'loon Toons	sound	2(chapter 5), 5(unit 2)
62. Seeing Sound	sound	2(chapter 5), 5(unit 2)
63. The Phonograph Balloon	sound	2(chapter 5), 5(unit 2)
64. The Talking Balloon	sound	K, 5(unit 2,chapter 4)
65. Model of the Ear	ear model	K, 5(unit 2, chapter 4)
66. Squeaky Voice	sound	2(chapter 5), 5(unit 2)
67. Charging a Balloon	static electricity	3(unit 5, chapters14-15)
68. Static Sticky Business	static electricity	3(unit 5, chapters 14-15)
69. Bending Water	static electricity	3(unit 5, chapters14-15)

Activity	Concept	Grade Level/Chapter
70. Gelatin Stalagmites and Stalactites	static electricity	3(unit 5, chapters 14-15)
71. Static Electricity and the Number 2 Pencil	static electricity	3(unit 5, chapters 14-15)
72. Static Trio	static electricity	3(unit 5, chapters 14-15)
73. Aluminum Can Races	static electricity	3(unit 5, chapters 14-15)
74. Anatomy of a Sneeze	disease	6(chapter 20)
75. What in the...?	inquiry	all
76. Egg Drop Balloon Experiment	inquiry	all
77. Water Lift	water pressure	1, 3, 4
78. Expanding by Cooling	physical change/properties	-
79. Dry Ice Magical Inflation	physical change/properties	-
80. Lung Model	lung/model	5(chapter 18), 6(unit 4)
81. Balloon Optics	refraction	2(chapter 6), 4(unit 2, chp. 6)
82. Whose Lungs Have Most Hot Air?	lung/model	5(chapter 8), 6(unit 10)
83. Whose Lungs Have Most Hot Air? Book II	lung/model	5(chapter 8), 6(unit 10)

Appendix F: Correlation of Activities with Macmillan K-6 Series

Activity	Concept	Grade Level/Chapter
1. Shhh! The Balloons Have Ears	air pressure	1, 2
2. The Stubborn Balloon	air pressure	1, 2
3. The Inside-Out Balloon	air pressure	1, 2
4. A Balloon Trick	air pressure	1, 2
5. Balloon in a Bottle	air pressure	1, 2
6. Betcha Can't!	air pressure	1, 2
7. Warming Up	heat	5
8. The Incredible Non-shrinking Balloon	heat	5
9. The Incredible Shrinking Balloon	heat	5
10. The Credible Shrinking Balloon	air pressure	1, 2
11. The Old Balloon-in-the-Bottle Trick	air pressure	1, 2
12. The Old Balloon-out-of-the-Bottle Trick	air pressure	1, 2
13. Hot and Cold	heat	5
14. The Soup Can Trick	air pressure	1, 2
15. Canned Hot Air	air pressure	-
16. The Puffing Jug	air pressure	1, 2
17. The Uplifting Experience	air pressure	1, 2
18. The Second Uplifting Experience	air pressure	1, 2
19. Balloon Cushion	air pressure	1, 2
20. Balloon Megalift	air pressure	1, 2
21. Son of Balloon Megalift	air pressure	1, 2
22. Son of Balloon Megalift: A Success Story	air pressure	1, 2
23. The Old Self-Inflating Balloon Stunt	chemical reaction	3, 6
24. The Other Self-Inflating Balloon Trick	chemical reaction	3, 6

Activity	Concept	Grade Level/Chapter
69. Bending Water	static electricity	4
70. Gelatin Stalagmites and Stalactites	static electricity	4
71. Static Electricity and the Number 2 Pencil	static electricity	4
72. Static Trio	static electricity	4
73. Aluminum Can Races	static electricity	4
74. Anatomy of a Sneeze	disease	5, 6
75. What in the...?	inquiry	all
76. Egg Drop Balloon Experiment	inquiry	all
77. Water Lift	water pressure	1, 2
78. Expanding by Cooling	physical change/properties	3, 5
79. Dry Ice Magical Inflation	physical change/properties	3, 5
80. Lung Model	lung, model	K, 5
81. Balloon Optics	refraction	4
82. Whose Lungs Have Most Hot Air?	lung, model	K, 5
83. Whose Lungs Have Most Hot Air? Part II	lung, model	K, 5

Appendix G: Correlation of Activities with Merrill K-6 Series

Activity	Concept	Grade Level/Chapter
1. Shhh! The Balloons Have Ears	air pressure	K, 1, 2, 5
2. The Stubborn Balloon	air pressure	K, 1, 2, 5
3. The Inside-Out Balloon	air pressure	K, 1, 2, 5
4. A Balloon Trick	air pressure	K, 1, 2, 5
5. Balloon in a Bottle	air pressure	K, 1, 2, 5
6. Betcha Can't!	air pressure	K, 1, 2, 5
7. Warming Up	heat	5
8. The Incredible Non-shrinking Balloon	heat	5
9. The Incredible Shrinking Balloon	heat	5
10. The Credible Shrinking Balloon	air pressure	K, 1, 2, 5
11. The Old Balloon-in-the-Bottle Trick	air pressure	K, 1, 2, 5
12. The Old Balloon-out-of-the-Bottle Trick	air pressure	K, 1, 2, 5
13. Hot and Cold	heat	5
14. The Soup Can Trick	air pressure	K, 1, 2, 5
15. Canned Hot Air	air pressure	K, 1, 2, 5
16. The Puffing Jug	air pressure	K, 1, 2, 5
17. The Uplifting Experience	air pressure	K, 1, 2, 5
18. The Second Uplifting Experience	air pressure	K, 1, 2, 5
19. Balloon Cushion	air pressure	K, 1, 2, 5
20. Balloon Megalift	air pressure	K, 1, 2, 5
21. Son of Balloon Megalift	air pressure	K, 1, 2, 5
22. Son of Balloon Megalift: A Success Story	air pressure	K, 1, 2, 5
23. The Old Self-Inflating Balloon Stunt	chemical reaction	6(chapters 3-5)
24. The Other Self-Inflating Balloon Trick	chemical reaction	6(chapters 3-5)

Activity	Concept	Grade Level/Chapter
71. Static Electricity and the Number 2 Pencil	static electricity	4(chapters 15-16), 5(chapters 12-13), 6(chapters 18-19)
72. Static Trio	static electricity	4(chapters 15-16), 5(chapters 12-13), 6(chapters 18-19)
73. Aluminum Can Races	static electricity	4(chapters 15-16), 5(chapters 12-13), 6(chapters 18-19)
74. Anatomy of a Sneeze	disease	3(chapters 15-16)
75. What in the…?	inquiry	all
76. Egg Drop Balloon Experiment	inquiry	all
77. Water Lift	water pressure	K, 1, 2, 5
78. Expanding by Cooling	physical change/properties	K, 1(chapter 1)
79. Dry Ice Magical Inflation	physical change/properties	K, 1(chapter 1)
80. Lung Model	lung/model	K, 1(chapter 2), 4(chapter 9), 6(chapters 10-12)
81. Balloon Optics	refraction	4(chapter 3)
82. Whose Lungs Have Most Hot Air?	lung/model	K, 1(chapter 2), 4(chapter 9), 6(chapters 10-12)
83. Whose Lungs Have Most Hot Air? Part II	lung/model	K, 1(chapter 2), 4(chapter 9), 6(chapters 10-12)

Appendix H: Correlation of Activities with Silver Burdett & Ginn K-6 Series

Activity	Concept	Grade Level/Chapter
1. Shhh! The Balloons Have Ears	air pressure	1, 2, 4, 5
2. The Stubborn Balloon	air pressure	1, 2, 4, 5
3. The Inside-Out Balloon	air pressure	1, 2, 4, 5
4. A Balloon Trick	air pressure	1, 2, 4, 5
5. Balloon in a Bottle	air pressure	1, 2, 4, 5
6. Betcha Can't!	air pressure	1, 2, 4, 5
7. Warming Up	heat	4(chapter 5)
8. The Incredible Non-shrinking Balloon	heat	4(chapter 5)
9. The Incredible Shrinking Balloon	heat	4(chapter 5)
10. The Credible Shrinking Balloons	air pressure	1, 2, 4, 5
11. The Old Balloon-in-the-Bottle Trick	air pressure	1, 2, 4, 5
12. The Old Balloon-out-of-the-Bottle Trick	air pressure	1, 2, 4, 5
13. Hot and Cold	heat	4(chapter 5)
14. The Soup Can Trick	air pressure	1, 2, 4, 5
15. Canned Hot Air	air pressure	1, 2, 4, 5
16. The Puffing Jug	air pressure	1, 2, 4, 5
17. The Uplifting Experience	air pressure	1, 2, 4, 5
18. The Second Uplifting Experience	air pressure	1, 2, 4, 5
19. Balloon Cushion	air pressure	1, 2, 4, 5
20. Balloon Megalift	air pressure	1, 2, 4, 5
21. Son of Balloon Megalift	air pressure	1, 2, 4, 5
22. Son of Balloon Megalift: A Success Story	air pressure	1, 2, 4, 5
23. The Old Self-Inflating Balloon Stunt	chemical reaction	3(chapters 5-6), 5(chapter 6), 6(chapters 5, 6)
24. The Other Self-Inflating Balloon Trick	chemical reaction	3(chapters 5-6), 5(chapter 6), 6(chapters 5, 6)

Activity	Concept	Grade Level/Chapter
25. Reversible Balloon	chemical reaction	3(chapters 5-6), 5(chapter 6), 6(chapters 5, 6)
26. Mmmm, Mmmm, Good!	chemical reaction	3(chapters 5-6), 5(chapter 6), 6(chapters 5, 6)
27. The Air We Breathe	chemical reaction	3(chapters 5-6), 5(chapter 6), 6(chapters 5, 6)
28. Float or Sink Balloons	density	4(chapter 5)
29. The Cartesian Diver	density	4chapter 5)
30. Hot Air Balloon	density	4(chapter 5)
31. Floating Balloon	density	4(chapter 5)
32. ...Like A Lead Balloon	gravity	3(chapter 6)
33. Gravity Balloons	gravity	3(chapter 6)
34. Bouncing Balloons	physical change/properties	3(chapters 5), 5(chapter 6), 6(chapters 6)
35. What Goes Up Must Come Down	gravity	3(chapter 6)
36. Balloon Races	gravity	3(chapter 6)
37. Comparing Gases	gravity	3(chapter 6)
38. Blowing in the Wind	gravity	3(chapter 6)
39. A Growing Line	physical change/properties	3(chapter 5), 5(chapter 6), 6(chapter 6)
40. How Did the Letters Grow?	physical change/properties	3(chapter 5), 5(chapter 6), 6(chapter 6)
41. Our Expanding Universe	universe	3(chapter 12), 4(chapter 11)
42. Air Has Mass	gravity	3(chapter 6)
43. Two Balloons in One	physical properties	3(chapter 5), 5(chapter 6), 6(chapter 6)
44. The Discrepant Event	air pressure	1, 2, 4, 5
45. A Piercing Moment	physical properties	3(chapter 5), 5(chapter 6), 6(chapter 6)
46. A Piercing Moment: Act II	physical properties	3(chapter 5), 5(chapter 6), 6(chapter 6)
47. Are Balloons Airtight?	physical change/properties/permeability	3(chapter 5), 5(chapter 6), 6(chapter 6)
48. Semipermeable Membranes	physical change/properties/permeability	3(chapter 5), 5(chapter 6), 6(chapter 6)

Activity	Concept	Grade Level/Chapter
49. The Spouting Water Balloon	water pressure	1, 2, 4, 5
50. Water Balloon Toss	-	-
51. Jet Propulsion	propulsion	1(chapter 6)
52. Zoom Balloons	propulsion	1(chapter 6)
53. Balloons and Marbles	propulsion	1(chapter 6)
54. Balloon Time	propulsion	1(chapter 6)
55. Balloon Rockets	propulsion	1(chapter 6)
56. Multistage Balloon Rockets	propulsion	1(chapter 6)
57. Rocket Boat	propulsion	1(chapter 6)
58. Air Power Soccer	propulsion	1(chapter 6)
59. Frictionless Air Scooter	propulsion	1(chapter 6)
60. The Balloon Squid	propulsion	1(chapter 6)
61. B'loon Toons	sound	3(chapter 8), 6(chapter 8)
62. Seeing Sound	sound	3(chapter 8), 6(chapter 8)
63. The Phonograph Memory	sound	3(chapter 8), 6(chapter 8)
64. The Talking Balloon	sound	3(chapter 8), 6(chapter 8)
65. Model of the Ear	ear model	K, 1(chapter 1), 4(chapter 14)
66. Squeaky Voice	sound	3(chapter 8), 6(chapter 8)
67. Charging a Balloon	static electricity	4(chapter 8), 5(chapter 7), 6(chapter 9)
68. Static Sticky Business	static electricity	4(chapter 8), 5(chapter 7), 6(chapter 9)
69. Bending Water	static electricity	4(chapter 8), 5(chapter 7), 6(chapter 9)